1)

THIS IS MY LIFE.

I am writing this book on a totally without prejudice basis!

This book is dedicated to you Laura,

My very special daughter who I love so very much.

The reason for the book is to allow you, Laura, to see my life and to know why I am the person I am today.
How the events of my child hood, my upbringing and the people closest to me have helped sculpture my life and have helped me to become the person I am today.

The events detailed in my book come from the memories I have kept hidden away in my mind and locked away in my heart for the past 40 years.
Writing this book for you will allow you to see how I was brought up and how I have become Me. Dad .PJ.

This will be the un-edited version and the truth; I would hate you to grow up finding out snippets of gossip from others who have "Selected memory", haven't got a Fucking clue and most of all think they know best and feel that they have to add little bits hear and there like a poor game of Chinese whispers.

I have not changed any names or protected any identity as I have nothing to hide and most of all nothing more to fear, as the book progresses the only people who have anything to fear are the people who made my life a living hell, I believe that revenge is a dish best served very very cold and karma dose exist.
Remember that these are my beliefs and the way I remember events as they happened, I don't judge people and also believe that everybody has a right to live there life in a way they think fit.

Always remember Laura, don't get mad get even.

Writing this book will also give me the opportunity of exercising some more of the ghosts from my past, the ghosts that haunt me by day and deprive me from sleep every night. It will help me in my search for the approval that I have desperately sought for the past 40 years along with helping me come to terms with the horrors that happened to me as a child.

My only advice to you is that if you decide to read this book, PLEASE remember this is my life and you cannot change the past, its events or things that have been said and done by others.
What has happened has happened. What has been done has been done.

But most of all Laura, please don't ask me how to deal with your emotions, the emotions that you will travel through as you step in to my shoes and progress through the first 40 years of my life.

I hope that you enjoy the book and most of all I hope that you now understand everything that has happened to me and why I am me.
I know that I am by far a perfect dad but hopefully you can find it in your heart to just accept me for the guy that I am.

When I started to write this book for you I honestly thought that it would be easy, a walk in the park, a piece of piss. Oh how wrong could I have been?
I suppose I am writing this book with my heart on my sleeve, it's a very honest version of my life and very blunt, Neither you or any body else will ever know the amount of time and effort I have put into this, but most of all the emotion I have gone through and tears that have been shed as I have re lived the most poignant times in my life, but please be assured of what a pleasure it has been to be able to do this for you, You will never know how proud I am of you and you will never know how much love and respect I have for you.

When you have a child of you own and the very moment the midwife hands you your child only then will you be able to feel the wonderful emotions that any a parent can feel,
Theses are my memories and some of the events may be in the wrong date order by a few weeks hear or there but all of the events are the whole truth and happened as detailed in the book as I remember them.

With all my Love, hugs, cuddles, kisses, squidges and squeezes.

Dad.xx

THE FIRST 40 YEARS.

December 7th 1965. A bitterly cold winter's morning and a baby deciding to make an early appearance into the world. Who in there right mind would leave the warmth of a protective womb to come into a cold and inhospitable world, but as every mother knows, when a child is ready to be born there is nothing to stop it.

There were a few problems of course. My husband was working a night shift at a factory several miles away and I had 2 small daughters asleep in their beds.

Once I was sure that the birth was inevitable near, I crept down the stairs and with a coat pulled close around me, I left the house, turning the key in the lock behind me.

Living on a main road, there was usually some traffic but at around three in the morning there was nothing, as I went to my neighbours next door but one and knocked on the door.

Realising that she hadn't heard me I looked about for something to throw at the window, all I had in my pocket was three pennies, they did the trick and having made sure that she knew who I was I signalled that I was going to the phone box down the road! A patrolling police car passing on the other side of the road and couldn't have failed to have bean aware of my pregnancy.

However they passed by, perhaps going some where moor important and I was left to go the phone box alone.

HORROR! It had been vandalised but fortunately I was able to get through to the operator who sympathetically listened and then took over, first a call was put through to the factory to alert my husband, next a call was put through to the hospital to tell them of our imminent arrival and then a call to the ambulance. It was a relief to have some one take over.

Getting back to the house I found my neighbour Bet Anxiously talking to two small girls who were sitting on the stairs crying whilst bet wondered what had happened to me.

Tears were soon dried and they sat and watched fascinated as she set about lighting the fire in the grate whilst I prepared for the ambulance.

By the time the ambulance had arrived the ground was icy and fog was forming, the cheerful ambulance men assured me that it wasn't the first time they had delivered a baby. This didn't reassure me at all, however I've always had a good sense of humour and I certainly needed it as the ambulance slipped and slithered its way to Manchester's biggest maternity hospital. There is always something cheerful about a hospitals admissions unit in the middle of the night. No matter how hard working, the staffs always seam so cheerful and in no time at all I was admitted and shortly after very relieved to hear my husband's voice.

Barley 3 hours later my son was born the image of his dad and perfect, what moor could we want?

A few months elapsed and with winter over, bet came to me one day with three weathered pennies in her hand. She had found them on her bedroom windowsill.

Some time after we left the district we kept in touch and bet treasured the pennies until 25 years later when my son, a young man was driving down the road where we used to live and as he passed the old house where we lived he saw an elderly lady stood outside the next door but one house, acting on impulse he introduced himself and was invited in and told the story of the three pennies, Bet went to the side board and removed a brown paper bag that had held its contents for the last 25 years. She handed him the bag and said, "These are for you" the contents of the bag held……………..3 old pennies!

Written by mum.

The first 10 months of my life were spent at 148 Moseley road Fallowfeild Manchester, we moved from there to 15 Fitzgerald court in Haughton green this was where Gran and granddad craven lived (my mums mum and dad) and where we stayed for aprox 2 months until we moved to our new home in Frederick Street, Denton Manchester

Allow me to describe my home and the place where I lived
As you turned off Ashton road in Denton into Frederick street the first building you came across was the dog and partridge pub on the corner of Ashton road and Frederick street next to it was Johnson's garage a family run garage that did general motor repairs, next door to the garage was Penelope ann., this was a factory that made children's

clothes, as you crossed the road there was a little corner shop on the right hand side owned by Joan fairest a white haired woman with a sharp tongue and attitude that would crack paint. She would charge you ½ a penny if you wanted your sweets on a paper bag (robbing bitch)
Across from the corner shop was Denton Working Men's club. Opposite the club was 22 Frederick Street a house that was owned by Betty and Alf and doubled up as a hairdresser. Next to the club was 11 Frederick Street a house that was also a hairdresser shop owned a run by Pauline berry. Pauline's husband Mell was a Coal man delivering coal to the local houses. Next to Pauline's house was 13 Frederick Street …….My home.

Our house was a typical 3-bedroom semi detached house it consisted of a hallway, a lounge to the front of the house a dinning room to the rear and a kitchen. Upstairs there were 3 bedrooms and a bathroom. Outside there was a small front garden with a drive that led to a dilapidated garage with a split-level garden to the rear, the garden was always full of roses, funny how 40 years later my least favourite flower is the rose.

My first memory of life at 13 Frederick Street was a wet Monday morning! , Standing on the armchair in the front room looking out of the window at the rain. I can see the rain running down the window, watching the rain drops join up with each other until they get so heavy that they run all the way to the bottom of the glass.
I suppose I would be about 2 years old at this stage. In the dining room to the back of the house we had a coal fire that had a back boiler to heat the water.

The room consisted of a table and 6 chairs under the window, on the windowsill was a wireless that played listen with mother on radio 2. I can't recall any other furniture in there but I know there was, I vividly remember the button box… I metal tin which contained loads and loads of buttons, if a button fell of a shirt there would always be a button in the tin to replace it, these buttons would also be used when we sat playing card games like chase the ace, we would use the buttons as lives and if you lost a game you would give a button up.

In the kitchen there was a gas cooker fridge freezer and a twin tub washing machine there was a large brown sideboard on the other wall and a few units above. In the side board there was the big brown jar of malt extract that mum took delight in giving us a spoonful every day as this was "good for you". The bathroom had a cupboard in it that used to be a kitchen cupboard it had a pull down front with glass doors at the top and wooden doors at the bottom, all the sheets, bedding and towels were kept in there.
Mum and dad slept in the large front bedroom and they had a pull cord light switch over the bed, I think they called it a lazy switch in those days, I remember being about 4 years old and taking the switch apart to see what was inside it and what made the light turn on the only thing I got out of my inquisitiveness was a humongous electric shock after sticking my fingers in the socket and a bloody good hiding for blowing the electrics.
Peter and I had bunk beds in the box room at the front and Colette, Kath and Anne had the large room at the rear.
Most of the walls in the rooms of the house had woodchip wallpaper, and I clearly remember in the darkness of the night I would pick at the small pieces of the chipped wood that was pressed into the paper on the walls,

Monday was wash day mum would get out the twin tub washing machine and wash all the clothes and dads bedding, when she had finished she would empty the dirty water out side in the yard put some jays fluid disinfectant with it and clean down the paths.

My next vivid memory of my child hood was going to play group.
My playgroup was at the festival hall in Denton I remember going through the heavy glass and wooden doors in to the main entrance then up the winding staircase that slowly curved at the top.
At the top of the stairs on the right hand side was a door that led to the playgroup run by Peggy Mather even now I can smell the polish, the smell of plaster seen and paint and I can hear the noise of children shouting and playing

I hated every minute of playgroup and can recall the many slept legs I got for having temper tantrums for not wanting to go.

Around the age of three years old I remember dad taking me to the place he worked.
He was a machine operative at Walls meat factory in Godley in Hyde, I remember having to walk from home to crown point in Denton and the getting the 211 bus which stopped outside dads works. I remember going through the glass doors, up the stairs and into a very noisy place, this was the sausage department where my dad worked. Even to this day I can still see the other people in white overalls and netted hats. And the look of pride on dads face. I treasure that look, as little did I know there would not be any moor
We came out of the factory and down the path, it was raining, we then went through a red wooden door, this was the factory shop I can still see the fridges with walls pies and bacon in them, dad bought us both a Funny face ice-lolly and we ate them as we walked to the bus stop to get the bus home. We walked over the little bridge and then on to the bus stop.
To date this is my only real recollection of having a DAD!! And doing things with my dad. Little did I know that my life was about to change? When I was 16 I got an interview at walls meet factory I said to mum that I wasn't sure where to go, she told me that I should follow my impulse, I got off the 211 bus in Godley and my feet carried me to the factory it was as if I was again 3 years old and everything was exactly the same. Unfortunately I did not get the job I went for but believe that this was due to the fact that when you are born you are given a pack of cards (I suppose the cards of life) fate plays the cards and as a human being all we do is shuffle the deck

My next recollection was my first day at primary school. St John fisher primary school, Haughton green. We caught the 127 or the 128 buses from the top of Frederick Street to Haughton green
It would cost us 2 pence in bus fare. Vivid memories of a black rubber bell strip I that ran above the windows and when pressed it would let the driver know you wanted the next stop.
I remember walking from the bus stop across the road I also remember the temper tantrum I had at not wanting to stay there and by the time mum had got to the gate I was there before her. Another round of slapped legs. Kicking and screaming and being made to stay in a place I hated……………I suppose it was like prison. Well to a 5

year old it was! As I write this I remember a television room at the school, it was a dark place and I remember a program that we used to watch. It was a cartoon boy. He was dressed in blue with a hat and in a playground where magic things happened. I.e. the roundabout, swings disappeared. ??? Don't know what it was but I remember it from 34 years ago.

Somewhere down the road we had to change schools. (Literally) we swapped schools with manor green school and ended up in a new school I vividly remember having to carry my own chair to my new school?? Something you may or may not want to look into.

After our move to the new school my first teacher was Miss. Blake Then it was Miss Pickering then miss Maguire then Miss Jackson and finally miss Renwick. I hated virtually every living day I spent at school. The head teacher was Miss Hampson. I beefy frightening woman who had a moustache and played the piano. When she sang she sang in a very deep voice and the words boomed out. She always seamed to where the same tweed type skirt, blouse and tweed waistcoat in a beautiful shade of tweedy brown.

By the age of seven years old my family was complete.........
Our family consisted of mum dad, Colette. Katherine me Anne and Peter. I have wonderful memories of coming home from school, and walking into the front room to see a carry cot in the middle of the floor, and there wrapped up in a blanket was my little brother peter. I remembered dad telling me that they had kept mum in hospital and allowed Peter to come home alone. Little did we know that mum was hiding behind the door in the dining room? When she came in the room we were all relieved, I remember sitting on the settee and mum putting peter in my arms to hold, he smelt new! (It wouldn't be for many many years that I would smell that newness again)

We were what you might call a normal family!!!!!! Hindsight. What the fucking hell is normal?
I remember a girl called Sharon muldoon .her family owned the unicorn wine store in Denton she seamed to spend a lot of time at our house I remember her changing peters nappies?? A little more useless info for you, I don't know what ever happened to her. Even at

this age I knew I was different to every body else. I just didn't know what was wrong with me.
To go back a little way by the time I was 7 dad was ill, he had had a stroke and well basically that was that by the time I was 9 he was worse. As I write this for you I find it so hard to put it
All down on paper, I think because a part of me doesn't want to remember the shit and the hurt we had to go through ……today is September 22nd 2004. It is a Wednesday and you are 10 years old we are on a Monday, Wednesday, Friday week. The days you stay with me. You are sat on the sofa. Playing with magnet x you will know what this is. Pieces of plastic with Magnets at the end, Ur fascinated with it! I watch from a distance hoping to god I am not fucking your life up to much. I dread so much that your life will end up like mine. I really don't want you to go through any of the shit and hurt I had to endure. Please god if you do exist allow me to be a good dad and make the correct decisions.

Think ive done a pretty shit job so far!!!

Today is Thursday 14th October 2004. Were on a Tuesday Thursday Saturday week is half-past six and your upstairs watching TV as I sit here and do some more work. Still worried that I might be fucking up your life. Just hope that what I am doing is the right thing

To get back to what I was saying

I said we were what you might call a normal family, looking back we were normal because this is what we knew and that was normal for us, from the outside and from others points of view we must of looked like a family of misfits who desperately needed a fucking good wash, clean clothes and proper food, I suppose a cross between the Walton's and the cast of little house on the prairie

Lets get back to being seven years old.

We all knew by this time that Katherine had been adopted as a baby, apparently her mother who was only 16 when she had Katherine They came from a "typical Irish catholic family who said that if the baby wasn't given up for adoption then they would have nothing to do with the Mother.

Mum and dad had decided to adopt a child as mum had had 5 miscarriages and was told that she would never have children again, On the day they went to court to sign the adoption papers mum also went to the hospital and was told that she was pregnant…9 months later I was born.

I remember that every Friday night we would be given our "spends" a 5 pence piece, and were allowed to go to the top shop on the corner of Ashton road and turner street, I would buy American cream soda, a sweet sickly sherbet, we would buy a mix up and crisp, funnily enough we would still have change.

Saturdays were really the same as any other day but with a bonus, we didn't have to go to school.

We all had our own jobs around the house, cleaning our bed rooms, washing and drying the pots and Cleaning down the kitchen surfaces, cleaning the bathroom and front room, setting the table for tea!! I hate that word! I can recall the list drawn up on the back of a cereal packet that hung on the back door with a piece of string it had the days across the top and our names down the side and in the middle were our chores for the day. But funny enough Colette still never seamed to lift one of her lazy idle fingers.

I hated Saturday afternoons as dad used to sit in the front room and watch sport, grandstand… he either watched football or wrestling, I remember the name big daddy, something to do with wrestling I took no notice of sport but the name is still there, At 5 o clock on a Saturday we had to keep quiet dad would still be watching sport and mum would be sat on a stool in the kitchen doing the football pools…I can never remember them winning.

I hated sport! Not sure if it was because I knew I was different from very one else or just the plain fact that no body took the time to show me how to play football or cricket or took time to allow me to be me. Sundays always started the same. We had to get up and go to the 11 o clock mass at St Mary's church in Denton. God it was boring. We had had to go the confession on the previous Saturday and confess all our sins to the priest; I was sure he always knew who I was so I sometimes disguised my voice and told him what I thought he wanted to hear. I would then end up with a penance of 3 Hail Mary's and 4 our fathers and told I should try to be a nicer person.... What bullshit I was 7 years old, what sins did I have?? Talk about being brain washed, Whilst in church mum would always put Ann and me on either side of her to stop us messing about, this didn't work as we would pull faces at other people in the congregation and end up in fits of giggles. This would usually end up with our legs being slapped. We had to go up to the alter and receive Holy Communion. A tasteless piece of wafer that stuck to the roof of your mouth and you had to prize it off with your fingernail, not very appetising to say the least. When the priest had told you it was the body of Christ it conjured up "disgusting thoughts"

After mass we would go into the church hall and have a cup of tea and a biscuit whilst the priest talked to all the parishioners and tried his hardest to prize even more money out of the unsuspecting suckers, I always remember he smoked a cigarette with a cigarette holder, if mum was in a good mood and there was only me and one other brother or sister we would have a mallow, biscuit pink or white mallow with a biscuit base and coconut on top.

The walk back home was usually hassle free. If we were lucky we would go past bardsley and hulse toyshop on Manchester road, in the window of the shop was a hornby train. You had to put a penny in the slot in the window to start the train it always fascinated me. I suppose it was because I knew I would never have a train set like it. We would walk along Ashton road past the blue star garage and the St John ambulance building we would play on the steps and climb the vertical bars of the labour club waiting for mum to catch us up eventually arriving home
On our return from church we would have egg and bacon or bacon buttes   mum would spend the rest of the day baking and we would play out in the garden with our friends.
We would play for hours with Marbles, and dobbers, skipping ropes and elastics. We had a variety of friends but our best friend was Wendy Burrows, Wendy lived at no 12 Frederick Street with her mum. Her mum and dad had split up and she had no brothers or sisters, through the years of our childhood Wendy virtually moved in with us, across the road from us at no 30 lived Albert and Audrey Seaton they had 2 children Darren and Abigail, at number 32 lived Mrs Walton and she had a daughter called Elaine. Elaine's dad had passed away and being honest Elaine was a spoilt brat. We used to play in highfeild street, the street opposite our house, we would use the 4 rain water

grids as bases and play rounder and French cricket with the other kids in the street but you could always guarantee that Elsie Walton would be out winging and complaining about banging the ball on the wall. Our house was always full of kids, mostly because as there were 5 of us and a few moor didn't matter but more often than not it was the parents who didn't want us in their gardens or houses.

I recall one Sunday afternoon, it was the middle of the summer holidays, we used to turn the garage into a den and sometimes mum would let us sleep in our den over night. In the garage was an old sheet boiler that no longer worked, we would fill it up with water and play for hours. Filling old jam jars and bottles up and playing shop. I recall the afternoon I went into the garage and took off the lid of the sheet boiler, inside there was some old foam as the young kid I was I had a fascination for fire, I lit some matches and threw them into the sheet boiler… horror… the thing burst into flames, I went into the kitchen and asked for a glass of water, I returned to the garage and threw the water onto the flames I expected them to go out but it just made it worse. After the third glass of water mum followed mum to the garage and put the lid on to smother the flames, after getting a "good hiding" I was sent to bed and stayed there until the next day

Mum baked everything. Bread biscuits buns filled with butter cream apple pies oat cookies and potato cakes and she also made her own jam, I think this was also another reason that the other kids in the area like to play in our garden because there was always fresh baking in the kitchen. We never had shop bought cakes or biscuits or even bread. Everything was home made but there never seamed enough to go around.
By 8 o clocks on a Sunday we were bathed, had our pyjamas on and were ready for bed. By 8 30 we were in bed. I didn't like Sundays at all as I knew school was next day. I wasn't particularly clever and the school work seamed very hard coupled with the fact that I just didn't fit in, I wasn't like any one else. I was different my clothes were shabby compared to other kids, my shoes were second hand and we just looked poor and we had a dad that didn't work and was ill. I was the odd one out. Due to being bullied at school I also wet the bed, I would wake most mornings to a wet bed and get slapped and shouted at for causing her moor washing, I suppose I must have smelt at school hence why the other kids in the Class picked on me; but I suppose smelling of stale piss was the least worry on my mind.

At play times I used to stand on my own in the playground away from any one else wishing that school would come to an end and the name calling and bulling would stop. to me this was a fucking hell hole, it was defiantly hell on earth and I was slap bang in the middle of it.

School dinners were something else, I recall having to line up in the hall, pick up a tray, knife, fork and spoon and wait to have our dinner served. Looking back I actually didn't mind primary school dinners. I used to love the curry and rice or the fish fingers chips and beans. Even a glass of hot chocolate, the only thing was is that we got free school meals, because we were poor, another piece of ammo for the other kids to use to bully me
At the age of seven I was confirmed at St John fisher church …moor religious crap I had to endure; the only good thing that came out of it was the party at the school after wards.

Most Wednesdays after school I Colette and Katherine would walk the half-mile or so from school in to Haughton green to the high-rise flats where Gran and granddad craven lived. You had to press the buzzer on the outside and we would be let in we then pressed the green button on the side of the lift you could hear the creaking of the lift as it stopped on the ground floor the door whooshed back and we were in we would press the button for the third floor and within no time at all the door would be Opened and we were on the landing, Gran and granddad lived at no 15 Fitzgerald court when you walked in the flat was always warm and had a smell of it's own there was a bedroom on the left as
You walked in, a closet and toilet on the right Grans bedroom on the left another store cupboard and the bathroom you would then go into the lounge and there was a kitchen just off it, gran's house was well furnished and had big windows. That looked out for miles, in the kitchen was a little cupboard and when you opened it there was a smell of shoe polish and potatoes, for tea we would have dairy lee triangle cheeses and square crackers granddad would sit in his chair and roll his cigarettes. I used to be fascinated watching him put the tobacco and paper in the little machine roll it through his fingers and hey presto a perfectly formed cigarette.

In the corner of the flat was granddads pride and joy his record player that played the old 78 records when you lifted the lid you were met by a wonderful smell. Sat here now I can still smell it.

I will never forget. Granddad put on the LP the sorcerers apprentice and would spend hours explaining to me the inns and out of what the music meant and who the characters were

They were what I would call fairly nice people. They had very strict rules .I suppose very Victorian values and that is where my parents got it. The only other thing was, like my parents they were very religious. Gran used to have a statue of the Virgin Mary in a glass case on the sideboard; she would light a tea candle every night and say a prayer to it. A bit bazaar I thought? She would put people's messages under the arms of Mary and tell us that when the little piece of paper fell out the prayer had been answered. Funny as far as I recall I never once remember any prayer being answered, I remember I used to go past the side board and stamp my feet in hope that one of the pieces of paper would fall out so I could tell her that one of her prayers had been answered and a miracle had happened, it never happened though I think that they were glued under the statues bloody arms and the only time they fell out was when the glue became that old and it perished.

Towards the end of my last year in primary school we went on a week's holiday to Babbercombe in Devon with the school. I suppose it was the first time I had been away from home, half of me couldn't wait to go away and get away from the shit at home but the other half of me didn't want to go and leave the dysfunctional lifestyle I had become accustomed to. I know this must seam strange to you but that's just how it was.

 We stayed at the Torcove hotel in Babbercombe and I had to share a room with a lad called Steven loco I didn't like him just like I didn't like any of the other kids that I went away with but true to form it was a week of hell. I still continued to be bullied and not just from the boys but the girls as well, the teachers didn't seam to like me either Mrs Salmon particularly didn't like me she would shout at me for no reason and whilst shouting her nostrils would flair like a distressed horse having an enema, she had a daughter "Paullina" who I hated and despised as much as her snotty mother she was one spoilt little bastard… and could twist her parents around her scrawny fingers whenever the mood took her.

Having spent 3 days in the hotel being bullied, picked on by the teachers and shouted at for no bloody reason I decided I had had enough, One morning I went up the stairs to the top floor where some of the lads who constantly picked on me were staying I put the plug in the bath and turned the taps on and went back to my room. Needless to say there was a fair amount of flooding and for once I didn't get blamed, it was like I had managed to get my own back with only me knowing, This is the first time in 30 years I have ever mentioned this to any one, well dose it matter now? What can they do now? Give me a bloody mop.

As the end of my primary school days came to an end I successfully failed my 11 plus exam, this only enforced the fact that I was the failure of the family, Colette had gained a place at the Hollies in Didsbury "a school for discerning young ladies" moor like stuck up cows who thought they were better than every body else.
I was told in the September I would be attending St Thomas more High school in Denton. Whippee!!! I cant fucking wait, but thankfully we have 6 weeks holidays before I have to even contemplate the next harrowing 5 years of shit and hell.

The summer of 1976 was one of the hottest on record with major water restriction put into place, there was standpipes put into the street so you could get water as the hot summer and lack of rain had made water levels drastically low the water was only turned on a certain times of the day and you would have to stand in line with the rest of the neighbours to fill buckets and bowels. A new couple moved into no 28 Frederick street Barry and Brenda, Baz worked at Lancaster carpets in Denton, but strangely enough I didn't really get on with him, all I knew is that he was mad about football and Manchester united and to be honest I hated football and any other sport for that matter. I would rather have my arms and legs ripped off by a rabid pit bull than play any form of sport.

As for Brenda I seamed to get on with her well. Over the next few years baz and Bren were to have 2 daughters, Kelly and Jody and eventually they would all have a profound effect on my life.
It must have been around 1980 when Allan and Carole Hines moved into 24 Frederick Street they were a young couple, Alan was a supermarket manager and Carole worked on the checkouts.

Peters birthday was on November 4th and every November the 4th we would have a bonfire party all the neighbours would turn up and bring fireworks and mum would make a pea and ham soup and we would bake potatoes and barbeque home made burgers and sausages, we would have a big bonfire in the back garden and burn everything that was around to burn, even the neighbours would bring old wood and stuff and in true Jenkins fashion we would have a fantastic party, the amount of fireworks was incredible and we would still be letting fireworks off well into the night,

It was on one of these parties that we borrowed a torch from baz and Brenda to enable us to see the mountains of fireworks that we had accumulated from friends and neighbours, it was only the day after when Brenda came to retrieve there torch that we had to inform her we had burnt it on the fire, they weren't best pleased but just accepted the fact that in our household these occurrences just happened.

I loved summer holidays getting up around 8am and sitting on the back door step eating hot buttered toast and listening to the birds singing, you could always guarantee that by 15 mins past 8 Wendy would be sat next to me eating toast and drinking a cup of tea. I always liked mornings, the best part of the day before any body could spoil it and fuck it up.
Wendy lived across the road at 12 Frederick street she lived with her mum and her Gran lived in highfeild street at no 6.Wendy's Gran worked at pollits, the sweet factory on wilton street in Denton and Wendy always had a supply of lollys with bubble gum inside and sticks of liquorish
We had very few toys so made our own games up and improvised using the things that were around the garden.
The back garden was on 2 levels and one of our favourite games was with a plank of wooden on the top level. 1 person would stand on the end of the wood nearest to the kitchen window and the others would stand on the other end the idea of the game was to pick a letter when the others stood on the plank you would rise up and look in the kitchen and had 10 seconds to count as many things beginning with the chosen letter… yea I know it sounds a bit stupid now but it kept us entertained for hours. We also played elastics and skipping and ball on the wall very simple games but that was all we had.

We used to play hide and seek, at times there could be 14 kids all playing hide and seek at the same time.
Across the road from our house at no 24 lived Sandra child, she had 2 daughters, Jackie was the eldest and then there was glenis, Sandra

the mum was what I would call a rough diamond, she had a variety of jobs, she had a taxi, she had an ice cream van but most of all her most favourite job was as a prostitute. We would spend hours watching and giggling at all the men that went in and out of the house, Jackie was just plain ugly with crooked teeth and glenis was a social misfit, she went to dale grove a special school for children who were just badly behaved, Glenis would climb up the drain pipe of her house on to the roof and do balancing acts on the roof whilst shouting abuse at us. She would throw fish fingers at us and tell us to eat proper food and we would throw a bar of soap at her telling her to get a wash. We even nicknamed her Bag wash.

Over the past few years dad's illness had progressively got worse and as well as being children we became carers. By now dad was quite bad, his eyesight was very poor his speech was poor and his hearing was none existent the constant whistling of his hearing aid did your head in, the numerous strokes he had had made him unable to walk properly and we had to do everything for him.

Dad was a big man. Over 6 foot in height and around 18 stone

The volume on the television was always at its highest and all dad ever did was sit in the chair and watch TV. All we ever did was look after him. Mum went to work Colette my eldest sister did fuck all, she would sit in a chair with her head in a book and never lift a finger if she was ever asked to do anything it would end up with the same old charade, she would pretend to have a migraine or a sore leg or a sore knee and as always she would get out of it.

She suffered with epilepsy and to be honest I think she put many of the attacks on, sometimes you would hear her having a fit in the night and we would laugh and say throw her in the bath and put the washing in there as well, you never new if it was real or just pretend, I had a distinct dislike for her only because she was 1 hell of a lazy , idle bastard.

Mum would go to work as a cleaner in the mornings in the club next door but 1 and would work behind the bar in the evenings whilst she went to work we would look after dad, most of the work load fell on myself and Kathy

The summer holidays were wonderful, the sun shone and we didn't have to go to school we didn't have enough money to go on holiday so mum would take us out for day trips. I remember 1 holiday we did go on, I suppose only because there are photos. I think it was abergely in Wales I remember it rained and rained and rained. Most of the summer holidays we would go out for days. We would visit all the parks Or take walks along the canals and mum would tell us stories, one day we went for a walk along the canal and had to pass through woodley tunnel as we started the long walk through the tunnel drips of water would fall from the roof, mum told us a tale that if any body ever fell in the canal and drowned the body would always turn up under the tunnel, as we got to the middle of the tunnel fear managed to get a grip it was pitch black and all we could see was a dot of light at the end of the tunnel by the time we were out and over the fright we would say that it wasn't that bad, But we never ventured there again.

Mum had a friend called Muriel Gilbertson they had grown up together and stayed friends all this time we used to get the bus to Levensulme and walk down the road to Fairborn road where Muriel lived she was very like mum in many ways the house was always full of home baked bread and muffins and cakes and she would always make sure we had a good meal.

I remember her husband John who was poorly and suffered with enforsemia, she had 2 daughters called Jean and Helen and a son called Billy when we went to murials house we would go to the park and play for hours. I remember I time I visited Muriel's house and I was given some bread dough to give to mum, I forgot that she had told me that the dough need to be placed in the freezer. When I got home I placed it in the fridge and thought nothing of it, it was only the next day when mum opened the fridge door did the full extent of my error become apparent. The dough had risen beyond belief and engulfed the contents of the fridge, and yep you guessed it I got a rollicking for it.

As the summer holidays came to an end we had a day out in Blackpool, mum and dad had friends who lived in Blackpool aunty Mary and uncle Ronnie (its funny how every body seamed to have an aunty Mary) so we would catch the train at Victoria station and make our way to Blackpool

The day was spent mainly on the beech and we would have paste sandwiches and orange drink made from powered orange crystals and added to water we would be given some money by Aunty Mary and Uncle Ronnie and we would go to the arcade and play the slot machines. We would go on the pleasure beech and go on the rides We would then make our way back to the station and make the long journey home with sticks of rock and sugar dummies

As the holidays come to an end we would make our way to "Sallies" in Denton, Sallies was a haberdasheries shop that also supplied school uniforms, as we were "poor" we got a clothing grant for uniforms, Black trousers, white shirt, black and yellow striped tie and a black jumper with a gold band around the neck.
I ended up with 2 pairs of trousers, 2 white shirts and a tie. I had a pair of black slip on shoes and a blazer, everything was to big for me but I was told, "I would grow into it"
I was told that Aunty Muriel would be making our jumpers. Muriel was a very good friend of mum and dads a little eccentric but a wonderful person. You always knew when the holidays were coming to an end when you had to get a new pencil case and pens and pencils

The last weekend of the school holidays were strange whilst writing this I have butterflies in my tummy

You will never know how many times over the past few months I have sat down and tried to continue with the next part of my life. But hear goes.

The nightmare begins

I remember getting up around 7.30 on the Monday morning feeling very nervous and very sick I didn't want to go to school!
I put on my new uniform that was to big for me and started the walk to school with Kathy, Kathy went to St Thomas more as well and had been there for the past 12 months, Katherine had already made friends so I felt alone.
I recall walking into the hall and being made to stand in a line at the front of the hall with all the other kids behind me and my new school "friends" I knew some of the kids as they were at St John fishers with me. …And most of them I hated.
The head teacher got on the stage and burbled in a Scots accent When he had finished and the assembly was over We were then told to line up at the back of the hall and our names were called out I was in Mr Dewhurst class and our form class was in the old maths room above the cookery room, when you walked in the room you could smell the stale smell of food from the cookery room below.

Over the next few weeks or so I kept my head down and didn't really stand out. I remember having to cover our schoolbooks in brown paper and remember that every body else seamed so much bigger than me and more to the point so much brighter than me.
We were told that we would be going swimming and that we would be having games and P.E. as I had no idea of sport I needed to make excuses for not doing these activities apart from that I couldn't swim.

All the teachers had been informed that dad was ill and that things were a strain at home, what they didn't know was how bad things really were. We would get home from school around 4.30 and more than likely sort dad out, everything had to be done for him, he had to be taken to the toilet and have his bottom wiped he had to have his food cut up and some times you had to feed him, he had to be bathed dried and dressed.
In the middle of the night he would fall out of bed and being the eldest son I would help mum to get him off the floor and back into bed, we had to give him his medication and basically do everything for him. You could see in his eyes the frustration and the humiliation he felt as we helped him with what we all take for granted.
By the age of 11 years old the dining room had been turned into dads room we brought a bed in there supplied from the hospital and a portable toilet funny how years before I had loved being in that room with the coal fire and the wireless, now I hate it.

As Katherine was already a pupil at Thomas moor school all the teachers knew about dad, One teacher took hold of the situation regarding dad, I was told that if there was a problem at home, if I was late for school due to a problem at home, if my homework was not done on time all I had to do was go to him and he would sort it out. For the first few weeks this was fine if I came in late, didn't hand in homework it was sorted. For the first time in a long time I actually felt that somebody was on my side.

I remember coming into school one day. It was about 9.30.my form teacher sent me straight to the teacher who was to "oversee" my problems; all the other teachers had no patience with me and told me in a very blunt manor that they would not give me any preferential treatment over the other kids. (Just for the record I didn't want preferential treatment, just to be treated like a human being.

I got to this teacher, knocked on the door and went inside I explained that I had been sent by my form teacher for coming into school late. The teacher who was sat in front of me got up from his chair and smacked me hard around the face.
He told me that he was sick of hearing all my excuses and having all the other teachers complain about me.
I was told to get out of the room and come back at the end of the last lesson. I walked out of the room in total shock I could not believe what had happened.
The person whom I had trusted and let my guard down with and who was supposed to help had turned on me, the rest of the day was just a blur.
I returned at the end of the day, shit scared of what was going to happen. I nervously knocked on the door and waited to be called in.
I went in, the teacher asked how my day had been I said it was like most other days I explained that I had to get home as dad was ill and mum would be worried as she had to go out to work I was told that if I had any problems I should just knock on the door. I was told I could go.
I left school very confused there was so much going on in my head I felt that my head would explode.
When I got home I was shouted at for being late home from school as mum would be late for work and dad needed feeding and getting ready for bed.

The next day in school we had games. I hated games and in a ploy not to do games I purposely left my games kit at home, I knew I was different and knew I didn't fit in and playing games or doing p.e only highlighted this.

My ploy didn't work and I was given an over sized pair of shorts and a ripped shirt and a pair of football boots a size to small. The other kids enjoyed taking the piss out of me to the amusement of the teachers we lined up on the football field. It was fucking freezing, and drizzling it was the beginning of October. Sir, chose 2 team captains and in turn the captains chose their best players, Yep…you guessed it the fat kid with the over sized borrowed clothes was last to be chosen.

They argued about how neither team really needed a liability on there team and this made me feel even more of the misfit I had become, in the end I was shoved on a team and put in the goal no end of protesting could get me out of it. The game ended bad we lost 5-0 and I was kicked and punched by the rest of the team for being a fat stupid freak that made them lose the game. I personally didn't give a shit it was their fault for putting me in the goal.

My punishment was to run twice around the playing field when I got back to the changing room most of the others were changed and gone but some were still there I was ordered by the teacher to strip off and get showered I shuffled into the shower and tried to get as clean as possible as quick as possible the teacher appeared and told me how I had let my team down the teacher then spent what felt like an eternity humiliating me in front of the remainder of my class mates on "how small my penis was and how fat I was, how I should be ashamed to call myself a human being and was a let down to my parents.
I left the showers got changed and once again was left mesmerised at what had just happened.
This teacher was supposed to look out for me not ridicule and humiliate me
The following day I made an excuse to mum that I wasn't well and stayed at home, mum didn't question the illness to much and it helped her out as well as she could go out shopping with out having to take dad with her.

On my return to school I was told to go to see my "teacher" as I had been off school without permission
I knocked on the door of his office and was called in, the room doubled up as not only an office but the teachers changing room as well; he had just got changed and was putting on his shirt ready to take another games class. I was asked why I was absent from school and I lied that dad was very ill and as mum had to go to work I had to wait for the doctor, in a very concerned manor he asked me how bad things were at home and how we were all coping as I told him I could feel the tears start to well up in my eyes and I blinked so hard so as not to cry as I stood there he put his arm around me and told me it was o.k. to cry.
I started to sob uncontrollable and as I did he hugged me and comforted me, for the first time in my life I felt I belonged and that somebody actually cared for me and understood about the shit we were going through.
He sent someone for some work and I was told that I should stay in his office until he had finished his morning lessons.

I spent the remainder of the morning in the tiny room carrying out my work and listening to the hustle and bustle of school life on the other side of the door, I felt privileged to listen to the coming and goings and at the same time feeling safe.

As lunch time approached I heard the changing room next door fill up with the excited noise of kids finishing there games lesson he came back into the office and locked the door he asked how I was I replied, ok and started to gather my things together he told me to carry on working so I did. He turned on the shower and undressed and got into the shower telling me that the water wasn't to warm. I recall general chit chat but nothing major, as he got out of the shower he smiled at me and asked me to pass him a towel as I turned to face him I could see that he was aroused he took the towel and grabbed my hand and forced me to touch his erect penis.
I froze! He pushed my head against the wall and whispered to me telling me to take my trousers down as I refused he gripped my throat harder making it hard to breath, I could feel the blood welling up behind my eye sockets and I thought that I was going to pass out.
I did what he said and took my trousers down he pulled down my underpants and started to touch me suddenly there was a knock on the door and he indicated me to get dressed I did and sat down at the desk with my back to the door. He got dressed and answered the door he bellowed at the kid on the other side of the door he closed the door and told me to get my things together as I got to the door he told me that if I ever told anyone they would take me away from my family and dad would have to go into a home and it would all be my fault.

I left the tiny room wondering what the fuck had just happened the remainder of my day was once again a blur.
I walked home frightened and confused and realised that I now had no one to turn to, my feet were sore from the football boots I was made to wear that were to small but this I could turn to my advantage.
I got home and was determined to do my homework so as not to have to go anywhere near him. I had to make sure that no one had an excuse to send me to him.
As I got ready for bed I washed and scrubbed my skin with the scrubbing brush in the hope to remove every last trace of what had happened at school I cleaned my teeth, on my little toe on my left foot the blister from the football boot was just going down I used the

pumas stone to scrub and aggravate the blister until it bled and continued to do this through out the night in the morning I showed mum my handy work denying any knowledge of how it happened I told mum I would call in to see the doctor, once again knowing that she had moor things on her mind she really didn't question my actions.

On the way out of the front door I riffled through mums coat pocket to find any loose change 88 pence later I was out of the door.
I walked and walked and at just after 9am I went to the chemist and bought some surgical tape I went to Audenshaw cemetery and dressed the toe as best as could with tape and gauze whilst sat behind a large grave stone so no body could see me carrying out me handy work I limped into the house and spun a tale that the doctor said I needed to rest my foot as it was infected it worked and I managed to get the rest of the week off school.
I don't know what was worse, time at school or time at home; life with dad was no bed of roses… being at home gave mum the opportunity of getting things done without dad under her feet but it also meant that I had to look after dad,

My return to school was petrifying; as I walked through the door my heart was pounding I still feel my heart beating now and the feeling today is just as terrifying as it was all those years ago.
I had a note from mum explaining why I had been off and to my relief the next week was uneventful. But even though uneventful I kept my guard high and tried to not get noticed

I somehow managed to get through the first year of secondary school life but on many occasions my mind had turned to suicide.

My next class was 2WE. My teacher was Wendy weaving she was the music teacher big fat and loud and to be honest crap at teaching music, her daughter was also a pupil Tracey weaving another spoilt bastard. With a blond bob hairstyle I can remember part of the register,
Philip baguly
Stephen birchall
John Boyd
Richard Edwards
Paul evens
Ged hone

John Hayward
Philip Jenkins
Andrew Lyons

I can't remember any more or choose not to; I remember less of the girls but hated every one of them apart from 1 girl. Amanda O'Brien she was also picked on but I liked her, I remember coming into school one day and our teacher told us that Amanda O'Brien's dad had died, I felt a rush of sorrow pass over me but strangely I also felt bitter that her dad has passed away who previously hadn't been ill, but my dad as ill as he was, was still hear, still ill and we still had to do everything for him. I suppose the word I am looking for is envious; yes I was envious of her. I know that it sounds a terrible thing but I have to tell the truth

Dads illness was getting worse he had spent a few weeks in hospital for some physio, when he returned things had changed one Monday morning as mum was doing the washing, betty, the neighbour at number 17 called mum over the fence to tell he dad was at the front door, after thanking her she managed to get dad back to the front room, telling him she would take him out in his wheelchair when she had finished the washing.

A few minutes later Betty again called to tell mum that dad was standing at the gate. , Again after getting him back to his chair she continued with the washing. A few minutes later a very hysterical Betty was again attracting mum's attention, when mum got in the garden she saw dad riding peters bike down the road and then falling off. The dustbin men had to get him back in the house, at the time it was awful but looking back it must have been an hysterical sight to see a grown man riding a seven year old bike down the road and falling into the gutter..

Later on that month we were sat in the front room watching TV mum had gone to the barcliff to play bingo, as usual the sound on the TV had got louder and louder over the course of the night, Katherine made a comment about how loud the TV was and dad seam to blow a fuse he shouted at Kath and started to get out of the chair both Kath and Ann ran up stairs and dad followed 3 stairs at a time.

They barricaded them selves in the bedroom but dad seam to have moor strength than ever. I ran up stairs and managed to get him into the bathroom where I had to keep him at bay with a brush handle. Peter ran to the barcliff to get mum. A few minutes later mum came

barging through the door. As she came up the stairs dad barged through the bathroom door and tried to push mum down the stairs, in one fail swoop she hit him on the jaw and knocked him out cold, we thought she had killed him.
We managed to get him downstairs and on to the bed. It took all of us to do it mum called the doctor and when he came an ambulance was called and he was taken back to Tameside general hospital. It turned out that he had been given the wrong drugs and if he had continued to take them for a day or so moor he would have been dead.

It was a Monday and as usual life at home started the same, I remember that dad had been up a lot in the night and I had got very little sleep
School was the same and I hated it, we used to go home for dinner as it was better for us (we had no money so mum would cook cooked cheese…grated cheese, with milk put under the grill and cooked eaten with a slice of bread and butter (absolutely fucking disgusting) I would put it in the same category as gruel from the Oliver twist film.

When we got home we were told not to make any noise as dad was poorly. I recall Kathy eating her dinner; mum called me and asked me to stay with dad who was upstairs. When I got upstairs dad was on the bed screaming with pain he was holding his head, I tried so hard to help but there was nothing I could do. Mum had gone to the club next door but 1 to phone for an ambulance I rushed to the club telling mum that she had to come quick.
When we got back dad was still in pain and screaming we were told to go back to school.
Both Kathy and I went back to school, both in tears I went to the staff room and got my form teacher to get my bag and returned home.
When I got home the house was empty and feeling scared and alone sat and waited to hear about dad.
A few hours later all the kids were home and Mell, our neighbour next door came to take us to the hospital. We were told that it was very possible that by the morning dad would be dead, as he had had
A ceribble hemmerage and was so poorly, we went into the side room where he was and dad was lying in the bed with machines everywhere

bleeping and clicking with tubes going in every possible part of his body, this along with the bleeps and bells, for a 13 yr old kid was horrific.
We spent the next few days at home worried and frightened to fuck. I had never experienced death before and the images that went through my mind were so very strange part of me wanted him to die so we could me "normal" but in the back of my mind I knew that I was still different and dad dyeing wouldn't change anything.

After a week away from school Monday morning loomed around again. We went to school with notes in hand explaining our absences I was sent to "my teacher"
I gave him the note and was told to take a seat in his office whilst he sorted out work for his class. He returned to the office and asked me what had happened. I started to tell him of the events of the Monday lunchtime and the tears followed. I tried so hard to stop the tears from falling but the harder I tried the moor I blubbered, he put his arm around me and told me that I was ok to cry and get it all out.
As I sit hear now I feel sick… he went from being a caring person whom I could trust to a person I did not know, he changed in the blink of an eye .i was thrown against the wall and he pulled down my trousers my head was in a spin I could hardly breath as the grip around my throat became tighter and tighter the smell of his cheep Brut aftershave clogging my nose and the weight of his body pressing hard against my body……………..

basically he raped me.

I was left in a heap on the floor crying scared and bleeding I was ordered to get dressed as he passed me he kicked me in the chest and I was told that if I told any one, I knew what would happen.
The smug look of satisfaction beamed across his face and the evil in his eyes cut through me.

Colette had been seeing a guy called David. Being frankly honest, I didn't like him, he was in my eyes a pompous asshole who like so many others thought he was better than every body else, he lived at cemetery house in denton, the house was in the grounds of the cemetery and was owned by Tameside council. His parents were very

old school and David was an only child hence why he was a spoilt bastard. I think I was about 13 when they were getting engaged, and on this evening mum had gone to David's parent's house to celebrate the engagement of her precious wonderful daughter and her daughter's new found love.
Mum had left the house and dad was sat as usual watching the t.v peter was pissing about and would not let me through the door. He would open the front door taunt and tease and when I went to push the door he would quickly close it, this charade went of for a good 15 minutes and my temper was failing fast as he opened the door and shouted out his toraide of names I pushed the door hard as he was pushing from on the inside my hand slipped and with my weight behind the door I fell through the glass panel of the door, the door swung back and I hit my head on the wall. All peter could say was that he was sorry. I went across the road to baz and bren's house and baz opened the door he looked shocked as I told him I had cut my nose, bren grabbed a terry towelling nappy and told me to hold it against my right arm baz went for the car and as we started to pull away from the house a large gathering of nosey neighbours had suddenly appeared around the house wondering what the commotion was.

I remember sitting in the hospital with blood all over the floor and the nurses telling baz that they were unable to treat me without my mums permission, they asked me where she was and all I could tell them that she was in the cemetery, they were puzzled and asked was she dead, I told them no she wasn't but she was having a party in the cemetery, they must have thought I was a bloody nutter and suffering sever concussion. Eventually I remembered David's sir name and within no time they had contacted mum and she was at the hospital, They started to clean me up and 68 stitches later I was sent home. When we got home mell from next door at no 11 had cleaned up the glass and put some plastic over the front door where the glass once was. When we got into the house dad was still sat in the front room totally oblivious to what had taken place. I had a few days off school and when I went in all stitched up it gave me some relief from the bastard who not only abused my mind but also my body.

For the remainder of my time at school the bulling from my so-called classmates and the teachers and the abuse from him continued. I was raped on a weekly basis sometimes 3 or 4 times a week.

Whilst it happened I pretended that I was somebody else and somewhere else to an extent I blamed myself as I believed that I had allowed myself to get close to someone and in return this was my punishment. I also believed that I was being punished for being "different" I distanced myself from these events in my life, the events and the mental torture that had become so paramount in my life and events that I could not tell anyone as the consequences would be catastrophic to the family I basically just switched off. He rapped me got his kicks and left me. I cannot be sure if I was the only kid this happened to, but I hope in a bizarre way I was.

I left school at the age of 16.

I was totally, physically and mentally fucked up .I was a mess.and still different from all the other lads in the class I now and had known for many years exactly what was wrong with me but hadn't a clue as to what to do.
But by this age I had managed to put on a face, the outside world looked on and not 1 solitary person apart from my abuser knew of the abuse I had endured or of the other burdon I was carrying around with me the burdon that was slowly eating away at me.
The parting words from my teachers were that I would be a no hoper and I would never amount to anything I was a looser and basically would always be.
I left school with 7 C.S.E exam results much to the surprise of the teachers and moor to the surprise of me. They were In history, geography physics human biology maths English literature, English language the grades ranged from 2 to 5s I know that they are a bit shit but at least they were mine, looking back I am so surprised that I even managed to get them but most of all no one could take them away from me...they were mine!!!!

I had been out of school 1 week when I got an interview with a gardening company. It was called Horticon landscapes and was based in Denton.
They contacted me 2 days later to tell me that I had got the job and started Monday at 8.am
My first day at work and I went to a place called Birchwood in Warrington. It seamed miles and miles away from home, there were

new housing estates owned by poco homes, Maunders homes and barrette homes

Our job was to weed shrub beds on grass verges at the side of the road; I was working with a guy called Brian calorhan he lived further along Frederick Street and new mum and dad fairly well. I liked Brian a lot and he taught me how to pace myself working and basically how not to kill myself in the process. over the next 12 months I felt that I actually belonged and had a purpose in life but deep down I knew that I was still different, I knew exactly how different I was and it scared the hell out of me I put the thought to the back of my head locked it away and made sure that it would never reappear.
Whilst I was working at Horticon there were too brothers who worked there Phil and Paul, we all got on very well most days we would work like hell in the morning and by 2 o'clock we would be in the pub. Looking back how we ever got any work done I do not know ,over the summer months I spent most weekends at Phil and Paul's house to be honest I preferred there house to mine I had to get away as I couldn't stand being at home. Dad was getting worse by the month and it only seamed that it was I doing any of the caring.

I remember Colette getting married, what an event! Dad was still quite ill at this time but the special day came and we managed to get dad ready only for him to wet himself a few minutes before the car came . I remember mum drying him off with the hair dryer.

After the wedding we went to the trough hotel in Audenshaw where the reception was being held. I didn't stay long I got a taxi to Manchester to Paul and phills house. I didn't really care for Colette and cared even less for her new husband David, he was what one might call a conceited twat he thought he was better than every one and from where we stood both Colette and David had got married on the rebound after previous disastrous relationships. But that was there shit and I didn't want anything to do with it.
On Friday January 13th I was made redundant from my job. We were called into the office just before 5 p.m and given our wages and told that our jobs were finished.
I walked home feeling gutted my job was finished and my income had come to a very abrupt end.
Within 2 weeks I had managed to get a job with Tameside council on the parks and gardens.

I had been for an interview and got the job. I was to be based at Hyde Park. My first day at work seemed very strange.
As kids mum used to take us to Hyde Park to play. It still felt a very big place and even though we had roamed the park as kids it now felt a much unknown place.

My first job was working with a guy called Steve brown we were tree planting on garden street in Hyde I enjoyed working outside I felt free. I was put on the outside maintenance team. Our job was to cut all the public open spaces, grass verges and old people homes in the Tameside area.
We had a charge hand called Len. He was a decent guy and let you get away with a fair amount of skiving. Within a short space of time you managed to learn all the fiddles that were going around.
Pay was based on a bonus scheme and every piece of grass you had to cut had a time against it. If you worked you socks off you managed to get your 50% bonus and have time to carry over for the next week.

Whilst working at Hyde Park this is where I first met Tim Bradbury. Tim was an undertaker who had premises on Wooten Street in Hyde, on break times or dinner times I volunteered to go to the local shop and would have to pass Tims premises, he would be stood at the gate with a fag in his mouth with ash all down his tie and jacket, he would always ask how things were going in the park and enquire as to how I was doing, I was surprised as how many people would stop and talk to tim and remind him that when they died not to forget to make sure they had clean draws on and where they could be found.
It was on one of these trips to the shop that tim stopped me and asked me would I like to earn a few extra quid helping him out, I was extactic at the thought of helping him, on all the occasions I spoke to him I would constantly be looking over his shoulder at the line up of coffins in his workshop, but I was also nervous as to what he wanted me to do.
He told me to meet him at his place at 2 oclock that afternoon, as it was a Friday we finished at the park at 1 it was no problem. I arrived at 2 outside Tim's undertakers and he was waiting in his estate car, I slid into the passenger seat and he was chatting about nothing important. He told me that we were just going to pick up a friend. We pulled up outside a house in godley, he got out and said he wouldn't be a minute, a minute or so later he came to the door and asked me to bring in the bag on the back seat, for the life of me I was unable to

find the shopping bag, as he came to the door he jestured to get the black bag on the rear seat, as I took hold of the bag and moved towards the house it suddenly dawned on me the ""friend"" was DEAD!!! And we had come to pick up the body, my legs started to shake and the butterflies in my stomach were flapping like mad,

I walked into the house and followed tim up the stairs, lying on the bed was an old guy who looked asleep, tim placed the body bag along side him un zipped the bag and he asked me to grab his feel whilst he got the head, I froze, on the table at the side of the bed was some socks rolled up, I grabbed a pair and put them on my hands grabbed his legs and put him in the bags, I couldn't get the socks off quick enough,
Tim told me to go down stairs and tell the lady to put the kettle on and turn on the radio, as I got down the stairs she told me that the kettle was on and that there was no need to put the radio on as she knew how steep the stairs were, I was mystified as to what was going on. I then realised that Tim was bumping the dead guy down the stairs, as they were to tight to bring the body down any other way.

We sat and had a brew whilst the wife went for his suit and shoes. Tim told her that he would call her in the week when he was ready for her. We put the body in the back of the car and started to drive away, I kept looking over my shoulder to Tim's amusement where he told me the guy wasn't going anywhere.
When we got the guy back to the undertakers we put the guy on the slab where Tim started to prepare the body. As I turned around the guy sat up and burped…fuck me I thought the fuckers alive I couldn't get out of there quick enough. I ran home from Hyde with my mind doing summersaults, as the fear took over I was sure that he was right on my heals I couldn't get the key in the door quick enough, slammed the door and went upstairs, lit a cig and tried to work out, what I had just experienced… a few days later when I passed the undertakers tim shouted me over and couldn't help laugh at what had happened. He then explained that the guy was dead and it was just trapped air in the body that made him sit up, the look of relief on my face made tim laugh even moor. I spent the next year or so helping tim out and enjoyed the work there, in hindsight I should have kept up the work and you never know might have ended up as an undertaker……….
But obviously that wasn't my forte in life.

Juggling work life and life at home was a constant battle, dads illness was getting impossible he was now so ill that every thing had to be done for him, he was having stroke after stroke most of them had been on the left side of his body so he had some use on the right side but the last 2 had been on the right side of the body.

Since the age of 15 I was lucky enough to be able to get into pubs without being challenged about my age. The down size of that was I was drinking heavy. I used to sit in the pub and go along the top shelf slowly getting pissed to
Drown out the problems of home and to drown out the problem I have been hiding away in the back of my mind for years.
November came and Anne had the bright idea of buying a puppy, as if there wasn't enough shit to cope with without having a bloody dog in the house. She called the dog Winston and along with the dog came the enormous amount of lies, " I will walk the dog, I will feed him and clean up after him, as usual she didn't and it fell to every one else to look after the dog.

As Christmas of 1984 approached there were the usual tensions in the house lack of money and the constant demands of dad's illness, dad had seamed to pick up a little and his constant request of doubling up on his drugs and his request for giving him moor tablets had seamed to cease a little.
Dad had a hate for the dog, whenever the dog went near him he tried to throttle it, I think it was due to the fact that the dog was getting the attention that dad used to get and he didn't like it.

January 5th 1985, a cold winters Saturday morning, the day started as usual getting dad out of bed taking him to the toilet getting him washed dressed and getting him sat in his usual chair facing the TV in the front room.
The Christmas tree in the front room looked pathetic, there wasn't a single needle on it and most of the tree lights had either fused or were just fucked after Winston had pulled the tree over on the numerous occasions since it being put up.

Mum was going out shopping with peter and Ann, Kathy was up stairs in her room so I decided to put dad in the back room whilst I removed the tree and cleaned up the needles, I threw the dog in the back room with dad to keep him out of the way. I spent the next few hours removing the tree and cleaning up the endless amounts of pine needles that somehow had seamed to bed themselves into the thread bare carpet.

I remembered that dad and the dog were locked up in the back room when I went in to the back room the dog was sat on dads lap
I smiled to myself, all I thought was that there were 2 lonely souls together I managed to get dad sat back in the front room and then started to prepare evening meal. I took out chicken thighs and cut the potatoes, 5 past three and mum and Anne and Peter walked through the door mum went upstairs to the loo and as I flicked the kettle on and picked up the cups to make a brew I heard anne scream for mum.

I dropped the cups in the sink and ran into the front room.
Dad was slumped in the chair, head back and his eyes were rolling in his head, he was a grey colour and his body was limp. Mum came in to the room and said we had to get him on to the floor; I had to pull him by his trouser bottoms to get him flat on the floor.
I ran to the phone, dialled 999 and asked for the ambulance, Ann was hysterically screaming as I tried to talk to the ambulance operator. I slapped her across the face and pushed her out of the front door to wait for the ambulance
On my return to the front room Pauline from next door followed me in she sat on the chair and held dads hand mum told me to give him cardiac massage and as I did I heard a rib crack, mum told me that I didn't matter as it would heal! I knew at that point that dad was dead but went through the motions any way; I also knew that if I gave him the kiss of life he would start breathing again but I made a conscious decision not to. Little did I know that my decision of that day would haunt me forever?

The ambulance arrived and the ambulance men worked on dad for what seamed to be ages they put him in the ambulance and mum followed she told me that she would ring when dad was stable.
I closed the door and Ann. Kath and peter went upstairs to try to take in what had just happened.
I returned to the kitchen and started to put the prepared food for dinner back into the fridge, it was like being on auto pilot I knew deep inside that dad was dead but something else told me not to be stupid.

I continued to finish cleaning the house when a knock on the door broke my trance. It was Mell from next door, he asked me would I give him a lift to get a door off as he was decorating and couldn't manage on his own.
When I got in to Mells house he told me that the hospital was on the phone and that dad was dead, I spoke to the sister at the hospital and told her I was on my way.

Mell drove us to the hospital and the journey was in silence. Once in the hospital we were shown to a room.
Mum was sat there along with 2 policemen, as we walked in mum told the police who we were and I was asked by the oldest copper was I the one who would be identifying the body,

I couldn't believe what I was being asked, for the first time in a very very long time I actually looked at mum properly, she looked empty, physically shocked and her eyes were red where she had been crying. we were taken to the mortuary and waited in a very nice room, to bloody nice to be honest with its clean walls and a picture hanging precariously from a nail on the wall and flowers arranged in white vase on a coffee table in the middle of the room, my heart was pounding!
I didn't want to see dad again, for the first time ever! the first time in my whole miserable bloody existence this nightmare was finally over, dad was dead and hopefully we could start to pick the bits up and get a life.
I know this sound so hard and unforgivable but you had to be there, every fucking day to witness the shit we went through, so as hard as this may seam to read please don't judge me Laura.
As we sat there numb and in shock and the reality of what had just happened had started to become reality and was now kicking in at a thunderous speed, I asked mum what was going to happen.
She told me that she would have dad brought home and kept over night in the front room in the coffin prior to the funeral. I was horrified that she could even think of this I told her that we lived there and she couldn't do that, she told me that we would discuss it on Sunday.

The deafening silence was abruptly broken as a door opened and a man in a white coat came out, I didn't want to see dad and even less didn't want to see a dead body that resembled a person who I knew and had done so much for.

I left the room and went outside where I borrowed a cig of the young copper who was stood outside. I remember coughing as the smoke filled my lungs I had used to nick the occasional cig of dads but having given up for about 2 years the thick smoke made me dizzy, the young copper gave me the contents of the cig packet and told me that he thought I would need them, I put them in my pocket as mum came out of the morgue.

Mel drove us home and the silence was deafening, no body spoke not even idle chit chat just the deafening sound of silence.

When we got home Colette had turned up with David, and as always was making the situation worse with her charade of pretending to be sorry and upset daughter who was morning the loss of a parent, as we got to the front door she demanded to know why I wasn't crying!

I simply replied that I had done everything for dad right up too the very end and she had not once lifted a finger to help him; I told her that her tears were tears of guilt and every waking hour she would be haunted by the fact that as a lazy lying deceitful spoilt bitch that she was who never lifted a finger to help him she would be haunted until her dying day, I think at this time I actually realised how much I resented and hated every inch of her pathetic body.

Over the course of the next few hours family who had never bothered before came crawling out of the woodwork, first Monica and Ronnie (mums sister and her husband) who were actually the only family members of mums who I respected then and still do to this day, and I don't have a bad word for them, they put Winston the dog in the hall out of the way. The doorbell rang and when I went into the hall Winston had shredded a new toilet roll all over the carpet, I picked up as much as possible and went to answer the door it was Joe and Lucy (mums brother and his wife) Joe was a nice guy but his wife was a stuck up twat she always looked down her nose as if we wernt good enough to breath the same air as her let alone be blood related.

The look of disgust on her face as she saw the shredded loo roll was a picture she just swanned in and perched herself on the edge of the chair not to comfy though, as she might actually catch something from the furniture

I borrowed £5 from mum and went for a drink in the club next door but one, I couldn't stand the hypocrisy. As I walked through the door in to the club you could feel people staring and whispering, passing false smiles of comfort as if they actually felt sorry for what had happened. To be bloody honest they didn't give a shit, they didn't have the time of day for him when he was alive and moor than likely just felt guilty.

For not doing anything for him
The only person who was actually genuine was a lady called Norma Lomas, she had worked with mum in the club for years and she knew how bad things at home really were, I remember 1 day asking her how I cooked some meet for dinner, she came in and showed me what to do but she was horrified that Colette was just sat on her fat arse reading a book and not bothered to help! but that was Colette for you. A lazy idle self centred fucking bitch right through to her black soul.

Sunday morning January 6th we all sat down in the front room and basically I made the arrangements for dads funeral, every one else just nodded in agreement and went either out or to there rooms to be alone with there thoughts.

Monday morning was strange; I got up and walked to Hyde Park where I worked. As I walked up the long path to the brew room, for the first time in my life I didn't have anything to worry about, I didn't have to think did dad have his tablets or was he ok or anything. he was dead and my mind was a blank.
The remainder of the week was filled with mixed emotions. Sorrow would just come over you and you would find yourself crying without warning the house seamed such a quiet place for the first time ever.

As Thursday approached the undertakers phoned to tell mum that dad was ready for her to come and see him. She asked me to walk round to the undertakers with her.
As we walked we didn't say much I told her if she didn't mind I didn't want to go in and see dad,she said that was fine.

We rang the bell on the door and a man opened it mum went in and I said I would stay outside with the living, he gestured by pretending to bite his finger nails that I was frightened and told me that it was the living I had to worry about not the dead he told me that I would be back. I think not I replied…
Mum came out in floods of tears .it upset me that I could do nothing to make the pain go away. All that was in my head was that if I had given him mouth to mouth he would still be hear and mum wouldn't be so hurt and upset. What had I done? It was my entire fault and the feeling of guilt was cutting into me like a knife.

Sunday morning 13th Jan 1985.

I had been up fore hours staring in the mirror trying to make the decision of weather I should or shouldn't go to see dad before the funeral tomorrow.
As I walked downstairs mum and Ann come through the front door, they had just returned from seeing dad in the chapel of rest, Ann said that I should go, I put my coat on and mum Ann and myself walked to the undertakers.
There was snow on the ground and my body didn't want to go through with the decision I had made but my feet kept on walking, mum told me that the dad I was going to see today wasn't the dad that died last week. I felt sick right to the pit of my stomach the same guy opened the door and he smiled a sympathetic smile as enough to say (see I said you would be back) I wanted to hit him so hard for being so fucking conceited, but most of all right.

I walked in to the room and slowly moved towards the coffin and stared down at my dad. Motionless and somehow different, all the lines of worry had gone he looked like glass and that if you touched him he would break. I asked mum to leave me alone for a few minutes I sat and spoke to him telling him how sorry I was for not giving him the kiss of life and saving him. I half expected him to sit up and say fooled you. But it didn't happen! As I left the room it was as if he was by the side of me I kept bumping into him .yea I know its stupid but that's how it felt.

Dad's body was received into St Mary's Catholic Church that evening.

Monday morning January 14th 1985.................. the funeral

I had had little sleep over the past week and just wanted today to be over.
I got up and put on my grey suit white shirt and black tie every one else was getting ready but no one seamed to speak to anyone else. there was a knock on the door it was ken freeman from broomstairs

nursery he had brought the flowers we had ordered, a 6 foot cross from us kids and a twisted red and white rose from mum.

I went upstairs and mum was sat on the bed crying I gave her the card for the flowers and a pen she just looked lost, by now family were turning up auntys and uncles that we hadn't seen for ages friends of mums and dads Colette and David arrived with colette in a black dress and black veil. She had to make sure she was the center of attention and that every one looked at her. Her dress had a split from the ankle to her thigh she looked like a slag.

As the car and the Hurst turned up the undertaker came in and told us that they were ready for us. Mum, Colette David me kath Anne and Peter were shown into the car I had never been in a funeral car before it smelt of polish and newness. As I looked in front of me I could the hearse filled with loads of flowers, I remember crying and being shouted at by mum, men don't cry she said now pull yourself together and dont show me up

We drove very slowly through Crown Point to St Mary's church, Once there we had a full requiem mass. After the service the coffin was taken out of church and put into the car. It was snowing now.

We drove up to Denton cemetery when we got there; there were around 100 people just stood around waiting to pay there last respects, and every one of them just looking at us. I felt angry that people just stared at us it made me feel like a freak!

As we stood around the grave farther cavey gave his words of wisdom and dad was lowered into the ground we were given a rose to throw into the grave and in true fashion Colette had to show the family up by virtually falling in the grave with the echoing words of my "farther my farther" you could hear the gasps of the mourners as they couldn't believe that even Colette could stoop that low. It was bad enough that she turned up to dad's funeral like a whore on heat but this took the biscuit.

We were taken back to the club and a buffet was laid on. The usual hangers on were in the club just waiting for a free feed at someone's expense.

The next 12 months seam to just pass, most of it in blur, and most of it blocked out by the amount o0f alcohol was consuming.

We managed to get a bit of a life but after 18 years of routine it was hard to break. I would still come down I the night to see if he was ok and to make sure that he hadn't fallen out of bed,
Only to be reminded that he was no longer hear. I still felt that the decision I had made not to give him the kiss of life was the wrong one. But somehow had managed to half convince myself that I had done it for not just our sanity but for dads sake as well. I remember only too well Ann once telling me sometime later that it was my fault that dad was dead as I should have given him the kiss of life. This hurt. It was like a knife being stuck in me. Ann by this time was training to be a midwife and her nursing training had given her a little knowledge. I knew that this was something I was going to have to live with and to make sure that it would not control my life.
My other problem had lain dormant for many months and I thought that I was now normal and it was just a phase but true to form it came back. It was now worse than before and I now knew that this problem wouldn't go away.
In June of 1985 I went to Romania for my first holiday abroad it rained and was cold and I hated every minute of it. I went with 2 friends, Wayne and Linda I quite liked them but Wayne was like a shovenist pig he treated Linda like a skivey.
I met pat and Eddie and Jayne and Trevor in this year and we seamed to gel, they lived in Uttoxeter and I must admit I spent many a weekend down at there house getting very drunk and enjoying there company. I was invited to Jayne and Trevor's wedding and even I must admit looked fantastic in a white linen suit, white shoes, lemon shirt and white tie, I will point out at this stage that it was not my intention to upstage the bride!
In 1986 I eventually turned 21. I had been seeing a girl who worked at the local bakery, she was called Marie she was o.k. But nothing special she was the first person I had sex with, it was bloody awful Fumbling around under the covers and I remember thinking is that all there is to it.
I had a party at Denton cricket club and invited every body I knew I had been seeing Marie for a while and to be honest I didn't like her but it sufficed, Phil had a girlfriend and was normal. I was very careful to make sure that the mask I put on every morning didn't slip.
My 21st was fantastic and I was centre of attention .
For the first time in my life I felt that I belonged and was normal, after getting very drunk we all pilled back home to mums house, I remember pat and Eddie was staying with eddies sister and brother in

law (Jayne and Trevor) they had the front bedroom and every body else slept where they fell asleep weather it be in the chair on a sofa or on the floor.

As Christmas approached so did dads 1st anniversary of his death, for the past 12 months I have lived with my conscience and for most of the time I have blocked it out of my mind with the help of alcohol,

I know that not giving dad mouth to mouth resuscitation was the best course of action and I also believe that anything other than the action I took would not have changed the outcome, but its so bloody funny how you always think that things could have been different, he might have come round, been able to talk walk and been ok, yea I know its only my conscience thinking that but ?????? .

My relationship with Marie continued for a while and to be honest I knew that she was just using me but to be honest I new that I was using her, every morning I made sure that the mask was in place and I could face the world,
I had started working at the Penny farthing pub In Denton I spent most of my time when not working in there so to get paid for it was a bonus, the landlord and landlady (Kevin and Leslie) were idle lazy bastards I have vivid memories of her telling me that when you did bar meals and you put the salad garnish on the side you could get 16 slices out of a tomato and 67 pieces out of half a cucumber, she was just out for as much profit as she could make.
I remember that Kevin used to refill the Guinness bottles with Guinness bought in bulk from the wholesalers to enhance his profit and pour back all the slops in to the cask mild and bitter beers, totally disgusting.

My relationship with Marie finally came to an abrupt end,

I found out that she had got pregnant and had an abortion!!
This mortified me, I know I didn't want to be a dad but I felt that a part of me had been ripped out and thrown away.
I really felt that I had been cheated and taken for a ride. And before you say it yes I know it was stupid…

The demons in my head came to the front and I went into a bout of deep depression I found it virtually impossible to keep up the persona

and keep the mask firmly in place, the things in my head wouldn't go away and my secret was sure to be discovered. I threw myself into work at the council where I loved being a gardener I was out in the open and felt free and not trapped,
Whilst cutting grass I would sort out all the shit in my head and go into my own little world, a safe place where no one would ever hurt me again.
My work at the pub was also a release I got to speak to people and whilst I was working it also curbed my outrageous drinking habits.

It was a Wednesday night in the penny farthing and the usual crowd was in there, for the past few weeks a group of girls had been coming into the pub and we always had a great night, on this particular evening they were all in and one of there friends was leaving to go to live in Australia so it was busier than usual and one of the girls Gill was as always on top form.

Something in life seamed to click and Gill and myself just became good friends, Gill was married to john and had a couple of kids Over the next 20 years Gill was to become 1 of my best and closest friends and my best critic and confident, little did I know that Gill would be onr of the people I would owe my life to.

Even though I threw myself into work the things in my mind constantly haunted me and deprived me from sleep. My mind became so confused that I needed to take things into my own hands, the only option was suicide.

I sat on the bed with a bottle of southern comfort and a bottle of aspirin, I recall watching the bottle lessen ¾, ½ ¼!!!!!
I woke around three in the morning sick all over the bed and myself and an unopened tablet bottle in my hand and was not sure if I felt glad or stupid, I didn't have a hangover as the amounts I had been drinking over the past few months had led to none hangovers, as always the nightmares I had disappeared and went to the box in the back of my head where I was determined they would stay.
Slowly, and as always I picked me up and started to put my life back on track.
It was Friday night and the penny was busier than usual The big chap in Denton was having a referb and many of its locals had descended

on the Penny, half way through the night three girls came in, two of them were sisters and the other was a friend of theirs. My shift finished around 9 so I set about talking to the three girls that had just come in.
1 of them was called Mandy she had the most fantastic eyes I had ever seen on any body

We got chatting and I had this flicker in my stomach I liked her and even though I had drunk too much we seamed to get on quite well.

A NEW BEGINNING

A week later the doors of the Big Chap opened and revealed a fantastic new pub the place was heaving and it was the place to go and the place to be seen the music of the "80s" was some of the best music that has ever been produced, my opinion any way.
Some of the guys who drank in the penny, drank in the big chap and over the next few weeks a group of around 15 of us used to meet in the penny on most Friday's, Saturday's and Sunday nights and then move onto the big chap, Mandy was one of the regulars along with Jackie her sister baby Janet, Paul, mike, Janet, Alex, Martin and many others no matter where we sat over the past few weeks I would always end up sitting next to or opposite Mandy, and little by little the rest of the gang tried in vain to push us together.

The second time I saw Mandy I spent most of the night crying on her shoulder about Marie and the abortion, somehow she didn't seem to be offended and actually helped me see things for what they were.

It was a Friday night and Mandy had managed to get hold of 4 tickets to see Oliver twist at the Palace theatre in Manchester Both Mandy and I, mike and Alex were supposed to be going but 1 by 1 the 2 guys dropped out leaving just Mandy and me to go alone. I asked a friend of mine sue and her boyfriend Dave to come along with us and that was my first proper date with Mandy.
I remember after the theatre we went into the big chap for a few drinks and I felt like I was on cloud nine nothing in the word could stop me feeling so happy and contented.
All the friends we had were in the big Chap that night all feeling pretty good that their match making had worked and we were actually going out on a date.

Over the next few months my relationship with Mandy got stronger and stronger and we started to see each other on a regular basis.
Mike didn't actually like me as I found out because he had a crush on Mandy, but hey that's his bag of shit.
Mandy had arranged for me to go to her mum and dads for Sunday dinner this was the first time that I was to meet them, to say I was nervous was an understatement, what if they didn't like me, what if they hated me??

We pulled up at the front of the house around 3 o clock and went in to the house I was introduced to her mum and dad and being honest really liked her mum, I wasn't keen on her dad but I thought over time it would get better.
In the week leading up to the meeting of her parents Mandy had asked what I did and did not eat I told her that I ate most things but didn't like tripe or trifle,
After small talk in the lounge we sat at the table and Mandy's mum had cooked a full Sunday dinner, for desert she had made a trifle!
I looked at Mandy in horror at the thought of having to attempt to eat trifle.
Trying to be polite I took a small spoonful of trifle and put it into my mouth, trying my hardest to swallow I could feel something hard. I pulled a piece of plastic out of my mouth to the horror of Mandy's mum and the amusement of Mandy and her dad, apparently whilst whipping the cream for the trifle a piece of the Wisk had broken off and as look had it I managed to get it. All I said was that if you didn't want me to come for dinner you should have said so; you didn't have to choke me with a piece of plastic.

A few weeks later it was a Friday night and Mandy picked me up from the top of the street, as we pulled into the car park of the penny farthing pub I got down on 1 knee in the car and asked Mandy to marry me she was a little gob smacked but she said yes.
For the first time in my life I actually felt that my life was perfect and all the bad things were now behind me.
We went into the pub and every one was delighted with our news somebody bought us Champaign and we had a fantastic night, Mike and his girlfriend nicki didn't seam to pleased but he was another that thought he was better than every one else and looked down his nose at me.

The following day we went to Mandy's mum and dads house and I asked her dad for his daughters hand in marriage, (I know it's a bit old fashioned) but I wanted to make sure that I did every thing above board.
After a 25 minute lecture on how special his daughter was and how I should never hurt her I was "permitted" to marry his daughter.

Mandy and I set a date of 17th June 1989 for the wedding.
We were to get married at   St George's church in Gee Cross

We held our engagement party in the big chap one Sunday afternoon and the place was packed with all the friends we had made.
We had to go to the register office in Dukinfield to have the bands placed on the board, as we sat in the waiting room people were complaining about a strange smell that had arrived, people were putting it down to the recent drain replacement work that was going on in the local area, we sat in the room with the registrar whilst she took all the details and even she apologised for the poultry smell that hung thick in the air, to be honest I couldn't smell a thing and thought nothing of it.
As we arrived home Mandy asked what I had been doing at work that morning. I told her that I had been helping dig a grave at Hyde cemetery; she looked at me in disbelief. its you she proclaimed " what" I said, it's you , the smell its that sweet sickly smell of death, that hangs around your clothes when you grave dig, I found this amusing as to be honest I couldn't smell a thing, I was made to strip off in the kitchen and put my clothes in the washing machine.

I had previously gone to see farther Cavey at St Mary's Church in Denton and asked him about what we should do regarding the bands he told me that as I wasn't getting married in his church and was marrying a Church of England person I should get out now.
I told him to shove it, followed by what a pathetic ass he really was, I finished off by telling him that it was ok for my parents to keep sending money to church every week but when I needed advice it was totally different I made no excuses about calling him the hypercritical ass he was and left.
The next 18 months were all work and very little play, Mandy's mum and dad had virtually taken over the wedding but Mandy and I had another plan. We would allow Jack and Carol to make the decisions on the cake , the menu, the flowers, the photographer the video the guest list and even the best man and bridesmaids, but un be known to them what ever decision they made we changed them to what we wanted.
I had been working for Tameside for a few years and I had got to be good friends with one of the grave diggers called Paul barns, both Mandy and my self had become good friends with Paul and his family, I had originally asked Mike to be my best man but that changed when

he took the piss out of me. I asked Paul would he be my best man and he was delighted,
Paul was what you could call down to earth, with a heart of gold. He was 6'2 tall and covered in tattoos but most of all carol and jack didn't like him. Mandy asked Jackie her sister to be her chief bridesmaid and asked Karen her best friend to be her other bridesmaid.
The venue was set the invites out and all was going to plan.

Over the months leading up to the wedding the strain of the wedding and work and everything else started to take its toll. We had been house hunting and as the housing market was through the roof, we had looked at house after house and nothing seamed to fit the bill.
Mandy' Gran and granddad called us to tell us there was a house just on the market, it was on Martin street in Hyde, the house backed on to the car park of the boxing club and was 2 mins from Mandy's Gran and granddads house we arranged to view the house and made an appointment for the Wednesday evening..
We got to the house, a terraced house 2nd from the end as we went in the smell of cat piss grabbed the back of your throat and shook your head, once we managed to get over the smell it was perfect , lounge with dining kitchen 2 bedrooms and a bathroom we decided to make an offer on our first home' the offer was accepted and we got the keys at the beginning of March.
I was involved in an accident at work in the January 1989 . and ended up with severe whiplash and problems with my neck and back, as the wedding got closer money got tighter, I was on sick and Mandy was working every hour god sent

We moved into our new house but Mandy being the good girl she was didn't move in straight away. Even though we were sleeping together she wouldn't move in until after the wedding,
 We had managed to collect quite a few things from the engagement and pick up a lot of other bits along the way so the house was virtually furnished.
Mandy's Gran and granddad gave us some money for our wedding present and we bought bedroom furniture with it.

June 1989 was to be one of the hottest months of the year, I had decided that our wedding was going to be the "grand affair that Mandy Carole and jack wanted, after all it was there youngest daughter and only the best would do.

1 month before the wedding' disaster struck, Paul my best man broke his leg and was in hospital, Jack found great delight in this and had already lined up a new best man.
As the wedding day came closer Paul was allowed out of hospital on crutches and out of plaster, we went to the hire shop that were fantastic and cut the trouser leg so that Paul could still be best man.

2 days before the wedding Karen Mandy's bridesmaid was involved in a car accident and Mandy's dad ended up with a bad leg and limping. Was it fated…………. Was this wedding going to go ahead?

I didn't manage to get a stag night due to all the upheaval but June 17th was hurtling faster and faster.
On the evening of the wedding I stayed at Paul's house and got little sleep at nine am we left Paul's house and made our way to my mum's house, there was already hustle and bustle with people getting ready and the every day hustle you would expect of a wedding day

Paul and I made our way down to Barry and Brenda's house where we were going to get ready, baz and Bren made bacon buttes and a cup of tea and we sat and chatted till it was time to get ready.
Whilst we were getting ready Paul managed to pull the shower off the wall and I managed to convince them it was my fault as always they were fine they were use to me breaking things and putting up with me.

We made our way back to mums where the wedding car was waiting for us, every one was dressed and looked fantastic, it was a startling difference from years before when we would leave the house as kids dressed in clothes that looked like the rag bone man had thrown out.

Both Paul and myself had full top hat and tails, we got into the car and made our way to Hyde Chapel in Gee Cross when we arrived there were already people there and more arriving by the minute the photographer started taking pictures of both me and Paul and by now the nerves were starting to kick in , before we made our way inside and took our place at the front of the church we nipped across the road to the grapes pub for a couple of quick vodkas, once the nerves were settled we went into church and we sat and waited for seamed to be for an eternity.

I still couldn't believe that Mandy was going to marry me!!

The music went quiet and so did the congregation then the organ kicked in and the vicar signalled to us to come to the front, as we stood there my knees were trembling the next thing Mandy was stood next to me and she looked amazing her dress was absolute gorgeous and she looked radiant, I felt a lump in my throat and I flickered my eyes constantly to stop me bursting into tears.

The temperature in church was well into the 80's and even the vicar had a pair of sandals on that made me and Mandy laugh. We went into the vestry to sign the register and for the first time since we got into church we had no eyes looking at us. I was nice to be able to catch our breath.
As we emerged from signing the register I felt like a super star, the flashes from all the cameras were blinding and continued until we got outside the church, the photographer continued to take what seamed like an endless amount of pictures and the fixed smile on my face was stating to hurt.
We made our way to the Oakland's Masonic hall in Hyde and prepared our self for the sit down meal. After the meal the speeches went without a hitch we got ready for the evening reception.

We returned to our new home as husband and wife and settled down to our new life together.
Money was tight as I was still on sick from work and to be honest I had too much time on my hands and in this time my brain started to think. The secret I was hiding came out of the box slowly over a period of weeks, it felt like it was getting a grip over me and I was loosing control, finally I snapped. After being out one Saturday night with Mandy I left a note on the table telling her how much I loved her swallowed the pills and washed them down with moor alcohol,

The rest is a blur; I woke up in hospital feeling like shit!!! They made me drink a mixture of charcoal to absorb the toxins from the tablets and made me wait till a shrink came and took me into a room for an "informal chat"
Would you like to tell me why you decided to kill yourself? He asked, I couldn't tell him about the demons in my head so in the only way I knew was to lie my way out of it . I told him about the accident at work and the whip lash injury I had suffered and convinced him that due to the amount of pain I was in things had just come to a head.

I left hospital with a letter in my hand from mum, telling me what a failure she must have been as a mother and how hard it was for her to see such a selfish sight. As in true mother fashion it was all about her , fuck me I didn't expect her to put her arms around me and give me a hug and ask if all was ok it was just how the fuck will the rest of the family see this and what on gods earth will the fucking neighbours say. God forbid woman you haven't got a bastarding clue of how shit and screwed up my life is and has been to date but don't worry mummy dearest I will do what I know best put it in a box and chain it up and forget it ever happened and pick up the shattered pieces of my life, dust me down, put a face on to the world and carry FUCKING ON.

November 1989 and my life of working for Tameside council was to come to an end, having been off work on sick for around 9 months I had managed to get a job a Peart engineering in Dukinfield as a collar and cap assembler I went into Hyde park on the Monday morning and gave in my notice to Dave Randall who was my supervisor, he told me that he had received a request from Peart engineering for a reference and had given me a glowing reference, he also told me that if I ever needed a job I should come to see him.

I went into the brew cabin to pick up my few belongings and above the seat where I sat they had pinned a note saying sick bay. Pathetic......

Pete ogen who was the park Forman, a small dumpy man who was set in his ways, who had a habit of scratching every one of his conceivable body parts whilst you ate your lunch stood up and told me that I was on light duties and would be litter picking and cleaning toilets in the park.

I told him that I didn't think I would be cleaning toilets or picking up shit left by other lazy bastards, he marched me to the office proclaiming that he was the bloody charge hand and what he said goes and if I though I was choosing what I was going to do I had another thing coming he got in the office and started shouting his mouth off at Dave Randal telling him that if he thought I could pick and choose jobs it wasn't going to happen , Dave Randal let him rant on until he ran out of steam, he calmly said that I had handed my notice in and as from 8 am this morning I was on a weeks holiday and that I was then going to finish,

Justice…. It was so nice to see that I had managed to wipe the smarmy look of his face.
I said my good buys and walked down the path towards home.
My 5 years at T.M.B.C was over and my new job and the next part of my life were to begin.

Janos………………………….

In the months I had been off work Mandy's mum, as always had been fantastic she would always look after us, she was for ever giving us money so that we could go out for a few drinks, she had kept a secret stash of money away from Jack the miserable sod she married , we still didn't get on and me being sick did me no favours.

Mandy's mum came to us one Sunday and gave us 15 pound,
she had won 30 pound on bingo and decided to share it with us.

Agnes in her wisdom had spoken to Mandy and convinced her that we should go to the dogs home and get a dog because it would be good therapy and give me something to keep my mind occupied

We went to Harper hey dogs home in Manchester, what a desperate place, rows and rows of yapping dogs all looking sorry for themselves. There was 1 dog that stood out from all the rest, he sat at the back of the cage not making a sound and looking very sad, a black and white mongrel, we called to him and sheepishly he came to the front of the cage, we decided that we would take him home.

All the way home he had is head out of the window as if he was trying desperately to clear his lungs and nose of the smell of the dog's home.

We got him home and he walked in had a good look around the house and sat down in front of the fire.

I decided to call him Janos it was a name I had heard from an actor called peter Lauri he played a character called Janos and the name just stuck.

Janos had been in the house 2 days and not barked; I couldn't believe we had bought a bloody dog that didn't bark.
Later that night we got into bed and Janos had decided that his place was to sleep at the bottom of the bed. We had been in bed about 20 minutes when we heard a car door slam outside and from the bottom of the bed we heard a little bark, both Mandy and I ended up in fits of giggles, when we woke in the morning janos had decided that he didn't want to sleep at the bottom of the bed on the floor but had managed to make his way inside the bed and was cuddled up between me and Mandy

We introduced Janos to Mandy's mum and dad and they instantly liked him, Mandy's gran and granddad loved him and spoiled him rotten and Mandy's gran told us that she would take him out through the day whilst we were at work, it was sorted.

Monday morning seam to come around quickly and my weeks holiday was over.
I made my way to my new job and the next chapter of my life.
By the time I had started work the word was already out that Jack leaver was my farther in law and he had helped get me the job.
My duties were clear I was to assemble cast iron collars and caps that were to be used by the gas board and the water board.
I was told categorically by the rest of the lads on the shop floor that I was to assemble no moor than between 180 and 205 collars a shift , I was told to go to the loo and waste as much time through the day as possible you could assemble 230 within a few hours but this way they managed to get overtime on Saturdays! Why the hell you would want to come in on a Saturday morning after spending a whole week inside a factory was beyond me.

By the end of the first 12 hour shift I asked Mandy to get me a new job . working inside was not my idea of fun. I hated it but it was going to be my job for the next however long.

The people I worked with were horrible, there was a welsh guy who they called taffy, a scruffy work shy arse hole who could turn laziness' into an art form and get an oscar for the performance and an Italian lad who I despised more than the rest, most of the people who worked there were institutionalised and could have been better placed in a centre for retarded misfits rather than an engineering company.

The 12 hr shifts I was working seamed like an eternity the only daylight I saw were when we went outside at lunchtime.

As we came up to our first Christmas we were looking forward to just me and Mandy spending our first Christmas day together.

We had some friends across the road Ron and Virginia Berry, Ron worked at Tameside council as a gravedigger and Vige worked in an office. All 4 of us got on really well and would spend nights at either there house or at ours.
 A few weeks before Christmas Ron was involved in an accident whilst working at a friend's house, at first they thought he had been electrocuted but later it turned out the he had a viral infection that had attacked his vital organs and he went into a coma. Over the next few weeks we would visit him in hospital look after his 2 boys whilst Vige went to the hospital, cook dinner and just be there for them, as Christmas day arrived our cosy Christmas day for two turned into Christmas day for 5, we invited Vige and the two boys over for Christmas day and served dinner and looked after them . Christmas came and Christmas went and Ron stayed in a coma. I would visit him every few days chatting to him and telling him the comings and goings of what was happening at work but nothing changed

It was mid February when one Monday evening I called to see Ron on the way home from work it was about 6.30 when I got there I had only been there a few minutes when Ron passed away.
By the time I returned the news of Ron's death had already been broken and we were all devastated.
We all new of the outcome weeks before Ron's death and Vige being the person she was had already been planning the inevitable, some

people may think that this is a callous act but its practical and I think moor people should take a leaf out of her book .

She arranged the funeral with Michael O'Brien of Murray's funeral services, Michael is a friend of mine, a really good guy who looks a little like Geoff capes, he has a heart of gold and is so gentle and polite it's untrue.

Ron's family were from New Mills in Derbyshire and were basically bloody strange, if not a little inter bread, they had not bothered to visit Ron any time whilst he was ill but now he was dead they were all mortified and putting on the bereaved relative act.

Vige came to Mandy and myself and asked if we would come in the funeral car with her, me to look after the 2 boys and Mandy to support her.

We accepted her invitation along with her request to make up the funeral flowers.

The night before the funeral Ron's family came down to vige's house and in no uncertain terms told Mandy and myself that we were interfering, we were mortified.

We couldn't believe that after all we had done these parasites were telling us to but out.

When we got home I still had the funeral flowers to do and to be honest I felt like saying stuff the lot of you.

I finished the flowers early morning, a 6' cross in white carnations with a centrepiece of red roses and foliage even though I say it my self they looked stunning, but there again I am good at everything I turn my hand to.

Vige came over to see us and apologised for Ron's family's outburst and pleaded with us to come to the funeral, she told us to just ignore them.

The funeral was terrible when we got to the crematorium the place was heaving with Ron's friends and family, as Ron had worked for the council for years all the guys from the council had turned up to pay there respects most of the guys there I knew well and had worked with, they couldn't understand why Mandy and myself were in the first car and taking such a front seat at the funeral.

I hated being stared at and people whispering behind there hands but its was what Vige had wanted, all it did was stir up the memories of

dads death and his funeral, the only up side was that this time Colette wasn't there to show not only herself up but every body else.
The funeral came and went and life seamed to slip back into "normal" mode. We would still call over every day to see Vige and the kids but one evening she didn't answer the door. We thought that she just wanted to be alone for a while. This happened on 4 separate occasions and then 1 afternoon we were shopping in Hyde and she just blanked us, I was upset to say the least and couldn't understand what we had done wrong.
It turned out that she had been sleeping with 1 of Ron's best mates at work for the past few months, even before his death, needless to say the friendship died a death and to this day I haven't spoken to her. Its not the fact that she was having an affair but the fact that after all we did for her, she has treated us like shit , I hate being used.

Life at the engineering works continued to be busy we were working 12 hour shifts and I still hated it, I got on with very few of the guys who worked there and the job was monotonous but most of all I detested working in doors I loved being outside in the fresh air where I could feel free and not trapped.

Sunday April 4th and we were working overtime at work there was a big stock take going on and as much as I hated it it paid well, I think the pay compensated for the boredom of the job and now realised that the money was the reason that the delinquents wanted as much over time as possible.

We had just sat down in the canteen when I saw Mandy's car pull up on the car park, I thought it strange that she was coming to work.
As she got out of the car I could see that she was in a terrible state and in floods of tears. I went outside where she announced that her granddad had died.
I was gob smacked! I went to my supervisor and told him that I had to go, he was a good friend of Mandy's dads so there was not a problem. When we got to Mandy's Grans house her mum and dad and sister were there they were all in shock and crying I gave Gran a hug but the reality had not set in at all yet, I asked where granddad was and was told he was on the sofa in the front room , jack came out and asked for his teeth, the undertakers had arrived I went in and he was curled up an the sofa where he had died then the reality hit me.

I stood in the back garden ,the sun was shining with a gorgeous blue sky , and all I could think was what a day to die and miss out on such a beautiful day, at that point the reality then hit me at full pelt and I broke down in floods of tears.

The next week was a blur coming to terms with granddads death and trying to console Gran.

The day of the funeral arrived and like most funerals it was not nice. To say goodbye to a person who you respect and have a lot of time for is a very hard thing to do, I would say that granddad was a perfect gentleman in every sense of the word.

Mandy and my self were making a good life for ourselves and getting on our feet. We had managed to decorate most of the house and even though money was tight we were doing o.k.

I had had enough of working at the engineering factory and noticed an advert for a gardener for Roland Bardsley builders in Dukinfield. I applied for the job and was told I could start the following Monday I went into work the following day and spoke to Les Hurst my supervisor, I gave him my resignation and although he wasn't surprised he understood my reason for leaving. I told him that working inside was not really my forte.
On the Friday just before I was leaving I went into the office to thank les for the job I was told that if I ever needed a job I was just to give him a call, I then set about telling him what the guys on the shop floor had told me when I first started, telling me that It was there policy not to do any moor that a couple of hundred assemblies a day as it secured there overtime.
He was livid, after all I had nothing to lose now but if they had treated me with the respect that was due and not constantly took the piss out of me I would have kept my mouth shut.

On the way out I made sure that I took the clock cards of the welsh twat and the Italian guy, well they had made my life hell for the past 8 months so a little inconvenience on there part was justice, and so what if they had to wait for there wages and be inconvenienced??

My first day at Roland Bardsleys was strange they had no Garden maintenance division in place what so ever so this was not only a new position for me but a new division for the company.

I was introduced to Alan, the Forman of the garage where all the company vehicles were maintained, I took an instant dislike to him , a little weasel of a guy with sly eyes and an a attitude to match.
His first words to me were if "R.B" asks you to jump you ask how high, I thought I don't think so pal.
I don't grovel to any one regardless of who they are.

I was approached by the head security guy a man by the name of Winston Walsh he was not only over all the security of the company but Roland Bardsleys right hand man he to was another sly person.

And defiantly a person you could not trust what ever you told him went straight back to Bardsley himself.

He introduced himself and told me that Mr Bardsley had arranged for me to go to Blackpool to his home, this was one of the maintenance jobs that we had to carry out every week.

We travelled up to Blackpool to bardsleys house.

A very impressive place in its own grounds, as we pulled up to the house the gates opened and we drove in. Mr Bardlsey came out and introduced himself. he took me round the garden and told me what he expected me to do. He told me categorically that I was to be at his house every Friday morning at 8 am prompt. Not five to 8 or five past 8 but 8 o'clock.

We then got in his rolls Royce and went into the centre of Blackpool where he owned the Ruskin hotel a 4 star+ hotel that was very impressive,

As we pulled up bardsley said " I will show you what power is" as we entered the hotel he bollocked every person in sight from the porter right through the kitchen to the chef and any one else that came in his way, when we exited through the back of the hotel he was very pleased with him self saying that was the way to treat your staff. All I could think was what a pompous twat…..

Over the next few weeks my role as gardener became even moor stronger with me having to advertise and interview staff and set up a complete maintenance and landscape division. I loved my new role and the pay was excellent. I was slowly learning the ropes and also how to work the system like the rest of the staff who worked there.

Working for Bardsley was an eye opener, every body was shit scared of him and when he turned up on site they ran like rabbits and disappeared into empty houses, on one occasion he went on to a new build site and sacked the complete workforce from the site manager down to the labourers and within a few hours the site was back up and running with new staff.

The majority of the work was keeping the show houses on all the new build sites in tip top condition, making sure that all the lawns on the empty houses on the site were cut and maintained to a high standard. I loved the work and loved the fact that I was my own boss really and no one bothered me.

I got a call from head office to tell me to meet "RB" on the Copley site in Stalybridge. I pulled up on site and a few minutes later the rolls Royce came around the corner, bardsley got out of the car and demanded to know why the grass on the last house of phase 1 had not been cut and was about 2 foot in height, I explained that the property had been sold and that once the sale had gone through it was the occupiers responsibility to maintain there garden, bardsley was having none of this and was ranting and raving. So I knocked on the door I knew the guy worked nights and when he came to the door not best pleased I introduced Mr Bardsley to the owner of the house and introduced the home owner to Mr bardsley and told him that he wanted to know why his grass wasn't cut . I then left them to sort it out.

Later bardsley told me that he was gob smacked at what I had done …I told him that he would get over it.

As the summer months came around my job was to make sure that Mr bardsleys house was full of colour and looked its best I was also responsible for making up the hanging baskets for not just his home but for the Ruskin hotel,
I set to work ordering plants and making up the baskets, I spent a full week at bardsleys house planting out the beds and making sure that the baskets were perfect, with all the bedding planted and the baskets up and looking good all I had to do was feed and water them.

By the end of September the house keeper at bardsleys home had informed me that Blackpool had a competition running for all the business and hotels in the area (Blackpool in bloom) and that the Ruskin hotel had won first prize for the wonderful bedding plants and baskets at the hotel and on the front page of the Blackpool gazette was a picture of Bardsley standing outside his hotel with a write up saying how he enjoyed making the baskets up and planting the bedding for the hotel.
I was gob smacked , to think that I had put all the hard work into the hotel and not got even a mention, on the other hand I was extactic to think that I had won first prize for all my hard work, it just proved that he was a first class twat.

My work at bardsleys continued and working in Blackpool became not only a joy but a get away from the office and all the back stabbing that went on.

We had decided to go on holiday to turkey in the August and the run up to the holiday was frantic I started to feel unwell and put it down to the hours I was spending at work, we were going away with 2 friends of Mandy's from the refuge assurance where Mandy worked(Tony and Laura) they were nice people and we got on well with them, 2 weeks before the holiday I was far from well and had to take 2 weeks off work, I had no energy, and felt like shit.

My boss told me to just take the time off and then go away and enjoy my holiday,
Even getting to the airport, was an event, I just didn't feel well and wasn't sure what was wrong with me.

We got to turkey and for most of the 1st week I spent little time in the sun and most of it in bed.
After a few days I noticed I had a few lumps on my chest and 1 or 2 on my back even though I don't get bitten we put it down to mosquito bites, but deep down I wasn't sure and new that it was more serious than a few bites from a mossy.
On our return from holiday I went to see my GP and told him about the "lumps" he showed some concern and told me that he was going to send me for a scan to see exactly what was happening, when he mentioned the word scan I started to panic he assured me that there was nothing to worry about and that it was only a formality to find the cause of the problem.

He got on the phone and phoned the hospital, there was a 8 week waiting list at Tameside general, 11 weeks at Oldham and 14 weeks a the Manchester Royal .
I asked how much it would cost to go private and would it make it any quicker.

It would cost me £240.00 to have a scan and a set of bloods done and they could do it in 3 days time.

I agreed and 3 days later I was sat in Christie hospital in Manchester having my bloods taken and awaiting a scan.

I was put under the scanner and afterwards told to take a seat and get a coffee until a consultant was ready to see me.

I was ushered into an office where a relatively young guy sat behind a desk looking at the results of my bloods and scan, I told him that he would have to talk in my language and not in medical garbage and that I wanted to no exactly what was wrong with me
Without a blink of an eye he told me that the scan showed I had 28 small malignant tumours
And that treatment had to be sorted ASAP.
My brain refused to take in what he was saying and I remember asking him exactly what he was talking about.
He told me in no uncertain terms that I had malignant melanoma or skin cancer.

The word cancer echoed through my head and I felt that my brain was going to explode with the information that I was taking in for a few minutes I lost the plot shouting and screaming at him that he must be stupid and I couldn't possibly have cancer of any such kind I was only young and in my mind 100% fit.

He sat there and didn't say a word until I had finished ranting on and on.
When I had finished he said shall we go for a walk there is something I want you to see.
We walked down corridors until we reached a ward full of children, as we entered the ward there were kids of all ages and most of them very sick , a young child came up to me in a base ball cap and asked me had I got cancer and was I going to loose my hair like he had he then told me that he was going to die soon and go and live with the angels in heaven.

I was horrified that this was happening and told Thatcher I needed to get out now.

The reality of my illness had hit me like a paving stone from a bloody great height, Thatcher told me that melanoma was a quick spreading form of cancer and if not caught soon enough was fatal, he told me that my cancer was treatable and I would have to come in on the

Monday to start my treatment, he told me that they could treat the tumours with laser and then a course of chemo therapy.
I left the hospital exhausted and feeling numb.

We had some friends coming for the weekend and I knew that I had to put a brave face on not just for me but for Mandy and our friends. Monday morning came and I told Mandy that I was going to the hospital alone. I needed to sort out my own head before I could sort out any body else's emotions.
Mandy picked me up from work about 20 past 5 and I got in the car and told her what had been said she burst into tears I told her that I didn't want to talk about it and that we should put it to one side for the weekend and take it from there.
The weekend came and went and every time I looked at Mandy I could see that she was in bits
I had a scan and blood tests and was then taken to a treatment room where I was to have laser treatment on the tumours on my skin I lay for what seamed for hours with a machine ticking and clicking over my body, killing the cancer that had attacked my body and if un-treated could kill.

Over the next week I under went a few laser treatments and then started a course of chemotherapy, I sat on the bed in a sterile bland and emotionless room and watched the liquid drip by drip enter my body I sat and waited to be violently sick waited for the moment I would loose control of my body and waited for the diarrhoea and cramps to kick in .
My wait was for ever , after all the liquid was gone apart from a bit of a temperature and a headache my side effects were nothing compared to the horrors I had read about and heard of , Karen my nurse told me that every body was different and took to the treatment in different ways, it depended on the strength of the cocktail of drugs that was pumped in to your body.
Going to hospital on my own and facing this on my own was something I needed to do. once I could cope with me being ill then I could cope with every body else, when people looked at me I could see in there eyes and by the expression on there faces that they pitted me. I hated that look I didn't want pity I vowed never to let this horrid evil thing beat me.

Around this time Mandy had informed me that she was pregnant. I was over the moon, to think that I was going to be a dad, within the space of 24 hours in my mind we had had the baby, saw it start school, grow up get married ect, I suppose that this something that a lot of people do, 13 weeks later the bubble was burst and Mandy miscarried. We lost our baby and were both devastated. I vividly remember sitting watching the scan picture desperately wanting to see a heart beat , the nurse looked at us both and told us that the baby was dead.
I cant put into words how those few words cut so deep and hurt so much, writing this now brings back that pain and sorrow I felt all those years ago, the only thing that helped was the fact that the nurse told us that is was mother natures way of saying that there was something wrong and it was natures way of dealing with the problem.

I left Mandy in the hospital who was to have a small op, I travelled home ,locked the door and got the gin bottle out, parents had been told and messages of sympathy had been left on the answer machine, My sister Colette called to tell me how sorry she was , lying fucking bitch!!!
She has no compassion for any one but herself. I sat on the floor and cried and cried and cried for the baby that we no longer had.

I picked Mandy up from the hospital the next day and little was said about the devastating events of the past 24 hours, I couldn't bear to go near Mandy Not that I didn't love her but I was so frightened of even trying for a baby again that I just turned off.
A few days after Mandy came home, it emerged that Colette had also suffered a miscarriage, and from the way it was described she had hemmerage all over the station platform on her way to work. She spent the next 6 weeks with her feet up on mums sofa….. This was just another blatant lie from her lying gob, she hadn't been bloody pregnant let alone miscarried, and she just needed to be centre of attention as per fucking usual.

True to form the deamonds in my head came to the forefront of my mind and my life like so many time before started to fall apart again I was convinced that it was "this" that was the reason for the miscarriage, was there a god or a higher being or was it karma that

knew the thoughts inside my head and this was my punishment for the shit that swam around inside it
.

Where we lived on Martin street, Ward street ran on the left hand side of it and about half way down just a few houses from where Vige And Ron lived was 2 young couples who lived next door to each other, they were both a bit odd one couple were relatively normal with 3 young kids and the other had a little girl who was downs, we nick named him the toy solider because he was in the territorial army and thought he was the best thing since sliced bread . I got on pretty well with both couples and the ironic thing is ,is that they were both called rob and Julie, so I with refer to them as rob and Julie and the Julie and toy solider,

My hours at bardsleys were long and by the time I came home all I wanted to do was sleep. For the past few weeks rob and toy solider would be sat on the front and in a childish way would keep setting the car alarm off to annoy the neighbours, after a week or so of this I asked rob who was letting the car alarm off as it was becoming annoying, he shrugged his shoulders and said he didn't know, as Friday night came around I was going out with Simon tailor for a drink as I got out of the shower the same car alarm was set off as I looked out of the window there was rob and Julie and toy solider and Julie laughing and pointing at me, in a fit of rage I flew down stairs with just a towel around my waist and went out of the door I asked him to stop setting the alarm off as it was annoying and he hurled abuse at me rob and Julie just laughed, and we all went in,

Simon and myself were in Denton working men's club having a few drinks and talking about what had happened previously, the moor I thought about it the moor annoyed and wound up I got , the more wound up I got the moor I drank, by the time I was going home I was furious,

As we walked past robs house he was at the window laughing about what had happened , I recalled shouting at the fat bastard to come down stairs and explain why he had thought it funny to shit stir, the next minute I fell against toy soldiers car and the alarm went off Simon ushered me into the house where I sat on the kitchen worktop drinking a large gin and tonic from a pint glass, the next thing there was a heavy bang on the door as I opened the door toy solider , rob and

another guy were on the doorstep shouting and screaming . all I recall was slow motion, from nowhere my hand clenched and with all my strength I punched the fat bastard in the face , my punch was so powerful that he flew 6 to 7 yards across the road and landed in a heap, the next thing toy solider and his mate had me pinned to the floor so that rob could kick the living hell out of me, Simon stepped in and held fat rob in a head lock and told them that he would let him go when they let me go , robs wife was shouting at Mandy to do something, Mandy had hold of janos so that he wouldn't kill any one and all the neighbours were out watching the performance within a few minutes it was all over .
It was decided that I should go to mums for a few hours to calm down when I got there I lit a cig off the cooker , didn't turn the gas off and set light to a tea towel nearly burning down mothers house, all in all not a good night.

The next week was uncomfortable quiet, no sign of toy solider or ugly Julie and no sign of Rob, the fat bastard I had hit, I can honestly say that he was only the second person I had ever hit in my life and I still to this day cant believe I did it. As the end of the week came to a close we finished at bardsleys and Simon (who was also working with me at bardsleys) went home to Tracey and the twins and I went home we had just sat down to eat when there was a knock on the door, I opened the door to find to coppers stood there " evening sir " he said can we come in, we are investigating an alleged assault that took place hear last Friday night and we were looking for some information, assault I said, there was no assault I told them that there had been a heated argument but that was about that, he asked me to call into the station any time Saturday to give my events of what had happened .

As I showed them out and closed the door Mandy said " told you it was to bloody quiet. I finished work around 12 on Saturday morning came home got changed and walked to Hyde police station, I told them my name and to my horror I was arrested on the spot, read my rights and put in the back of a police car where I was taken to Stalybridge police station, all that was going through my head was I hope no one sees me in the back of this car. When I got to Stalybridge cop shop I was taken to a desk asked my name date of birth age address ect I had to empty my pockets and take off my belt and give them my shoe laces I was then taken to a cell and the door closed behind me. There was another guy in the cell and the first thing he asked me was " what u in for pall" I told him alleged assault, he said did you hit him, my first thought was that they had placed this guy in hear to trick me and catch me out, I said I hit no body mate haven't got a clue what there talking about, I asked him what he was in for he said Murder. My heart skipped a few beats and I smiled thinking FUCK ME he started banging on the door and shouting the officer in charge. The door was opened and he demanded a cig, the officer asked him dose your mate want one to… Mate I thought I don't even no the guy and I am no mate of a guy who is in a cell for murder, as I finished me cig the door opened and I was taken into an interview room where to coppers were sat at a desk, in half relief I recognised one of the coppers from the big chap where I worked, be fore we start Phil he said if you hit this guy tell me now and I can get you off with caution, the words came out from no where I haven't hit any body, they stared the tape and then started to ask me questions about what had happened on the Friday night. I lied, blatantly lied to the police why, I don't know. I just did.

I was released on police bail to return in two weeks at 7 o'clock on Sunday night, I was then shown the door and free to go.
I called Mandy and told her of the ordeal I had been through and asked her to pick me up from Stalybridge Mandy picked me up and I told her what had happened, that night we were going out in to Leigh with Mandy's friends Tony and Laura when we got there I told them what had happened and every corner we turned there seamed to be a copper standing there I thought they were following me .

The next week was odd I went to work as normal and kept a very low profile when I came home I stayed in side and didn't answer to door, I went to a solicitor and showed them the charge sheet and asked him why I was having to return on a Sunday night in 2 weeks time he told me that they would keep me in a cell over night and I would be in court on the Monday morning to face charges of assault, my stomach churned, he told me that if found guilty I could spend 3 months in prison or receive a fine along with court costs as I had no previous convictions.
Now 3 weeks prior to all this happening on a Saturday afternoon Robs wife Julie came over to our house in a terrible state, she was crying uncontrollably Rob had been arrested with reference to him flashing at some young girls, she also mentioned that something had happened when he was 17 regarding the same thing, like the person I am this

stuck in my head and all Mandy and myself could think is that if he has a record of this from being 17 then it must be true.

The end of the week came around so quickly it was Friday night and Mandy had gone to her mum and dads house to see to the dogs as they were away and were coming back on Saturday,
I was getting changed when there was a knock at the door I peeped out of the window and saw 2 coppers at the door half of me wanted to hide and the other half wanted to let them in so the nosey bloody neighbours wouldn't see them I thought shit that's it they're coming to arrest me and take me a way my mind was frantic as the second knock on the door echoed through the house janos was barking like mad so I opened the door and asked them in. janos was snarling at the two of them and they asked me to lock the dog in the kitchen,
We have spoken to rob and his wife regarding recent events he said but she is still adamant that they press charges he said. He then told me that they had been told that recent events with his own arrest would also come in to the conversation.

A glimmer of hope shone into the room I said to the older copper is that regarding him flashing at kids a few weeks ago, the younger copper said yes but they didn't have any concrete evidence of it, the older copper told him to shut up, he then told me that they had decided to drop the charges and if ever there was a dispute I should call them and not take matters into me own hands, I still stood by my stories and told him that I didn't hit any body, as they were leaving he said to me "the next time you hit the bastard make sure that he doesn't get up, as people like him should be castrated, true to form I said I didn't hit any body.

As they left I closed the door and relief fell over me. I can't believe I got away with it. Not just hitting him but laying to the police, this tort me a lesson don't take matters into your own hands. AND DEFINATLY DON'T LIE TO THE POLICE.

When Mandy came in I told her of the events that had happened and like me the relief was over whelming
Not long after we put our first home on the market and started to look for a new place to live.
We had grown out of our first home and the people , apart from a few were nothing but common.

This is the bit that will make u laugh, there had been a new guy who started at Bardsleys whose name for a minute escapes me he was a sly ass hole who couldn't be trusted he was brought in to work along side me but within 2 weeks had taken over completely and I new that I was being pushed out to make way for the new guy and his creepy son, he had the way of doing nothing made in to an art form and could have had an Oscar for the little amount he did but for the way he pretended to do everything. He took an instant dislike to me and within a week I had been made a scapegoat and both myself and Simon were sacked for gross misconduct, to be honest I didn't care as I had enough on my mind. will I be alive in 6 months or will the cancer have spread and become untreatable

I spent the next 3 months unemployed and recovering from the after effects from the treatment I had been through along with feeling sorry for my self and the possibility of going to prison.

I had been out of work for around 3 months and hated every single minute of it,
The 2 weeks before I had noticed a job for a gardener in the local job centre based in Marple in Stockport. It was to work on private and commercial gardens within the Marple and surrounding area,

I took the bull by the horns and enquired about the job, an interview was arranged for the Wednesday afternoon.

I went up to Hibbert lane in Marple and met a guy called mark Bradley; he had run his own gardening business for around 10 years and was looking for a gardener to assist.
I told him of my experiences with the local council and the work I had carried out for bardsleys I told him of the machinery I had used and that I also had a clean driving licence.

I left marks house with a job!! I started the following Monday and the relief of having a job was wonderful I must admit at this stage that working for mark was not all it was cracked up to be when it rained and we couldn't do any work I would be paid a pound for turning up to work. The work was easy to me, as I had always done it, the hardest thing was learning my way about, as I didn't have a clue where I was in the Marple area.

As my new job progressed in started to get to know my customers and I think most of them liked me , mark was a funny guy we could work all week and the only words he would say to me were you cut the lawns or you hoe the beds, we talked very little sometimes and that I found hard, most mornings I would make my way to his house and knock on the door and he wouldn't be out of bed.

We eventually got a buyer for 49-martin street and were still looking to find a new home,
We came across a house in booth street Denton no 52, it had belonged to a couple for around 30 years and the place was very run down,
We put in an offer and awaited with baited breathy to see if it was ours, with our offer accepted we started the process of moving and awaiting for all the legal shit to be sorted
As August approached Mandy informed me that she was pregnant. With all the turmoil of the miscarriage we decided that we would tell no one and just carry on as before.
To be honest I said to Mandy, just tell me when you have had it.
I needed to protect me from the pain that was so vivid from loosing our first child.

52-booth street became our new home and at last we had a garden and a house that needed a lot of work we were close to our friends, Gill and John, ellen. Alan and Carole. And we had a new baby on the way.

We spent the next few months sorting out the house and getting a builder in to put new windows in, to put a porch on the front of the house, to build a conservatory to knock down walls and put a new kitchen in.

The builder told us that the work would take a few months and the whole house would be ready by Christmas.

The builders moved in and we moved out for what should have been a week, we stayed at Mandy's mum and dads house I returned after a few days to find we had got no floor boards the builders had decided that instead of repair the old floor boards they would rip them all up and put new ones down in there place, a ploy to get moor money out of us. We ended up staying at Mandy's mums for 3 weeks, as

Christmas approached the work on the house seamed to get worse before it got better as Christmas eve approached we threw up the Christmas tree set the table and prepared for our first Christmas in our not so finished new home. Bare floorboards and unfinished work every ware but we got through it.

By the end of February the work was nearly complete and Mandy was getting bigger by the day, even the blindest person could not have mistaken her for being pregnant.

By the end of March the house was completed completely decorated and looking like a show house.

Saturday April 2nd and we think that Mandy has gone into labour, we contact the hospital and they tell us to come in. 25 minutes of being attached to a monitor they tell Mandy that she hasn't gone into labour and send us home.

Sunday April the 3rd and by lunchtime Mandy is once again attached to the monitor at st Mary's hospital and once again we are sent home being told that baby has turned and is just bedding in ready for the inevitable birth,
We return home a little deflated and then go the Mandy's mums for Sunday dinner, we have come a long way with her Sunday dinners they come without pieces of broken Wisk now. ☺

Mandy spent most of the dinner pushing her food around the plate saying that she didn't feel hungry we decided to go home. Around 6 .30 Mandy sat in the lounge and burst into tears I felt useless I told her to go and have a hot bath to ease the back pain .she snapped back "if I have another bath I will look like the whale I feel I am" I called Ellen, if any body should no what to do it would be her. She came around and just gave Mandy a hug she picked the phone up and called the hospital, she very calmly explained the situation and asked had any body actually read Mandy notes. She told them of the miscarriage and told them that as Mandy had never got this far in a pregnancy the told Ellen to tell us to once again come to the hospital.

As we arrived on the ward we were met by a midwife called Amanda Fox, She shook my hand and then put her arms around Mandy and gave her the hug that she needed, Before Amanda could say anything

Mandy said in between sobs of tears I know the room at the end to be put on the monitor.

We sat for what seamed like an eternity watching the monitor beep and beep little by little printing out heartbeats of baby. Amanda came in and told Mandy that she was going to do an internal to see how far dilated she was after the examination she told us that Mandy was going no ware as she was 4 centimetres dilated and baby was slowly on the way I was told to go home as I would only be in the way. I said my goodbye to Mandy and was told that they would call me when Mandy was ready for me. I drove home in a nervous sort of daze, I sat at home and Kathy Pete and Joanne came to keep me company around 11.30 Pete and Joe went home leaving Kath and myself alone. Around 2.45 in the morning the phone rang, as I answered the phone, put my shoes on and coat on all at the same time the nurse told me that Mandy was now ready for me to come to the hospital . I shot out of the door, got Kath in the car and drove to mums house, virtually throwing Kath out of the car without really stopping.

I flew down Hyde road at about 90 miles an hour when in the mirror I saw the blue lights of a police car and the siren blaring , split second decision, do I stop or do I carry on.

I pulled over and the policeman asked me was I in a hurry? "well actually I am I said my wife has gone into labour" at witch hospital he asked taking my driving licence from me, " St Mary I said Indignantly" he went to the car and got on the radio he came back gave me my licence and told me to follow him, When we get to the cross roads at the a6 just follow me.
With sirens blaring and lights flashing I was escorted to the hospital, a police motor cycle had stopped the traffic at the A6 cross roads and waved us through, I pulled up behind the police car and he gave me a ticket to put on the windscreen as I was parked on double yellow lines, he then called me back and I thought Shit.he is going to book me .. he gave me a piece of paper with his number on and told me to call him to let him know what we had had.

As I got to the front of the hospital the porter was waiting for me the policeman had called the hospital to check my story the lift was waiting for me and 12 minutes from receiving the call from the nurse I was on the ward with Mandy, Bloody hell they said .I told them of the police escort and the events of the past 12 minutes.

We were taken to the delivery suit and waited for events to happen, Mandy was given some pain relief and we chatted and joked with Amanda fox and her junior, I fell asleep for an hour or so . it was 7.30 am on bank holiday Monday 4th April 1994. the sun was just rising over the city centre , I remember thinking what a wonderful gorgeous day to be entering the world.

The deliver suit was prepared and Amanda asked was I ok . I told her I needed the loo and a quick breath of fresh air when I returned to the ward Mandy's contractions were getting closer and closer I was flannel monitor mopping not only Mandy's head but my own.

At just gone 12 20 a nurse came into the delivery suit and said that Mandy's mum was on the phone, I picked the phone up and Carole asked how Mandy was I told her that she was asleep and that probably baby would be born later that evening, I told her I was going to get a bite to eat and would call her as soon as anything was happening. I put the phone down and the nurse very puzzled said to me, " I don't think you understand Mr Jenkins, Baby will be born very soon, I smiled and said to her " do you really want Mandy's mum under her feet flapping about? She smiled at me at took me back to the delivery suit.

As I returned it was all quite frantic Mandy was pushing and pushing she moved from being on all fours to lying on her back, as a bloke I felt useless, watching Mandy in pain and not being able to do a thing about it. Amanda the midwife was fantastic she told us that she could see babies head and wanted Mandy to give one big push in a matter of second the head was out followed by the rest of the body she announced that we had a baby girl is was the most awesome sight, watching this lifeless baby slowly turn from a grey motionless object slowly turning pink, The cord was cut, the airway cleared and then the most wonderful sound in the world the first cry of our baby daughter. you weighed 7 lb 14 oz and were born at 12.46 you were wrapped in a towel and it was announced that all fingers and toes were present and you was perfect, Amanda turned to me and said we will just let dad hold you whilst we sort out mum as she gave you to me and you smelt new ! a smell I hadn't smelt since I held my baby brother all those

years ago. I held you, my baby daughter and the tears started to flow, uncontrolled crying of happiness and the relief we had a perfect daughter and the fact that I had just witnessed the closest you will ever get to see a miracle happen, as I write this now I feel the exact same emotions as I did all those years ago the tears are flowing and I write this with the gift off hind sight I have the most wonderful precious daughter in the world.
As I sat there holding you, no army in the world could have come between the two of us.
In the background I could hear Amanda fox saying to Mandy "is he ok. Mandy just replied .yea, that's Phil for you.
They had delivered the after birth, the doctor had checked you and your Mum and all was ok. I was somewhere on cloud nine I was so proud …..I was a dad, but most of all I was so glad I had a baby girl I didn't want a boy …………… I didn't want it to turn out like me!!!

Still inconsolable Mandy phoned her mum and dad and phoned every body else I was to busy blubbering to be able to speak to any body.
We had been looking at names for months and decided to chose a name that wasn't easily shortened, we decided on Laura Jayne, little did we know that over the next few years you would be known as Laura, lo, Lois Loz lowie and any thing else abbreviated.
When I looked at you, you had a mass of jet-black spiky hair, the comical thing was is that you had moor hair than me.

Within 20 minutes Mandy's mum and dad had arrived at the hospital and were revelling in the thought of being grand parents.
I called the policeman shortly after to let them know about the arrival of our baby daughter and a few hours' later flowers and a congratulations message arrived from them.
Over the next few days I visited the hospital as much as I could I would bring in strawberry's and cream and home made sandwiches in for your mum ,much to the envy of the other mums on the ward, they would tell there husbands what Mandy's husband had brought in and the look of I think embarrassment on there faces showed.

A few days later we were ready to take you and your mum home from the hospital, my mum had arranged to be at our house to make sure that the kettle was on and that the house was warm,
I arrived at the hospital and you and your mum you were ready to come home we thanked Amanda fox and all the staff and put you and

your mum into the car. When we arrived at home Janos went berserk, he hadn't seen your mum for a few days and was ecstatic to see her, my mum busied her self in the kitchen and I took you around the house to show your new home. Telling you about each and every room and taking pride in showing you your new room.

I took you into the lounge and undressed you apart from your nappy I placed you on the changing mat in the middle of the floor and to the horror of my mum I brought Janos into the room I told janos that this is Laura and you had to look after her and I told you that this was janos I then left you both in the room and closed the door be hind me , I watched janos as he licked you from head to toe.
My Mother was fuming, "you cant leave the bloody dog alone with a baby she shouted it will bloody kill her" she said, Mandy and myself assured her that it would be fine.
5 minutes later we went in to find janos lying by the side of you , you were 100% intact and had come to no harm as we had predicted.

We knew that by doing this Janos would always protect you and you wouldn't come to any harm when he was around,

We soon settled into our new roles as parents and the house was always full as everybody wanted to come and see our gorgeous daughter .

We had decided that we would have a very big christening party for you and we set about making the arrangements for your christening

 I remember the first time I took you out in your pram on my own I walked you to the corner shop to get some cigs and felt so proud at the people who stopped to have a look and a poke at my new daughter. I left you asleep outside the shop whilst I went in, moira and Jeff who owned the shop went outside to see you and we stood chatting for a few minutes.
I had got half way home when I realised that I had left you outside the shop. Well I wasn't used to pushing a pram was I ? let alone having a baby to look after

I raced back to the shop and you were still there and still asleep, it then dawned on me that there was more to this parenting lark than I thought I then realised that you had not only changed my life but turned it around, upside down and inside out all in one fail swoop….all in a good way though.

At the beginning of May 1994 Mark the guy who I worked for told me that he was fed up with the gardening business and asked me if I wanted to buy the business from him.

I was gob smacked, the thought of running my own business was something I had dreamt of for years but never thought it would become a reality, I sat and talked it over with your mum and she thought it was a great idea.
It was decided that I would rent 20 gardens from mark and pay him a percentage of the takings. To be honest it was a bit of a piss take as the rent was fairly high but I was now the proud owner of my own business,
Your mum and me decided that we were going to have you christened and set about putting all the plans into action. A lady in Frederick street club by the name of jean was a dressmaker and I asked her would she make your christening robe. I wanted it to be very over the top and very glamorous but most of all very special as you were the most precious little girl in the world.
We had made an appointment to see farther John at St Hilda's church in Denton; we were unable to have you christened at st Anne's church as the vicar had left.
We called up at 7 o'clock on the Wednesday evening just as they were bringing a coffin into church.

We waited outside until all the people had left and went inside to see farther John pouring a large whiskey into a glass and the drinking half and throwing the other half over the coffin. He said that she had always said the he must have a drink on her….. I found him a little bazaar but accepted it as it was.
We decided on a date and then went to Stamford house to arrange the reception after wards.
I wanted to make sure that every body knew how gorgeous you were and how proud me and your mum was.

Prior to your christening your dress had been made and it was gorgeous right down to the shoes, all hand made and hand stitched.

We had been out one Sunday and had only just got in when the phone rang it was grandma Carole on the phone, I heard her talking to her mum and getting upset, Carole told Mandy that jack had left her and was having an affair, we were gob smacked at what we were hearing. We got into the car and went to grandma carols house she was upset and crying Jack was at his mum's house in Nelson Street where Jackie was with him.

As your christening came nearer Grandma Carole told your mum that her and jack had got back together. I told your mum that the only reason he had crawled back was to be able to come to the christening, we decided that we needed some space and that we didn't want to see him, we made sure that we took you to see grandma at every possible time but made sure that he didn't see you, I actually despised him, this is a guy who I had looked up to and trusted and he had indirectly betrayed my trust, I really like Carole and she had always looked after me and your mum, but I hated him.

The day of your christening came and we dressed you in your new christening robe and you look stunning we walked to the church where our friends and family were all there waiting, grandma carol and "he" arrived but couldn't make any eye contact with Any body, he was like a little boy who had been caught steeling sweets, he looked embarrassed and pathetic as the pathetic person he really was.

After the service we made our way to Stamford house and had a wonderful celebration, uncle peter made a speech to welcome you into our family.
As I stood up to give my speech the tension in the air was thick people were worried about what I was going to say. But in true form this was your day and I made no reference to "him" what so ever, I didn't even give him eye contact.
I made sure that every guest there had a picture taken with you when I got to take a picture of grandma Carole and him I made sure that I said to Carole that hear is your granddaughter and made no reference to him at all. I will never forgive him for the hurt he caused your mum let alone grandma Carole

We left Stamford house after having a wonderful day our precious daughter was now christened and everybody shared our joy.

6 weeks later on a Saturday afternoon the phone rang and Mandy answered the phone, I heard her scream down the phone a asked her what was going on I picked the phone from her and jack was mumbling on the phone he put the phone down when I asked him what was going on.
Mandy told me that he had asked her to pick her mum up from work and tell her that he had left her for good.
As predicted I was right he had just crawled back to attend the christening. He was nothing but a sly spineless bastard, who was to spineless to even tell his own wife that he was leaving her and had to get his daughter to do his dirty work.
Mandy went to the market hall to get her mum, Carole was surprised and Mandy said that her dads car had broke down and she was picking her up.
As Carole got in the car Mandy told her what had happened and grandma was mortified. They pulled up at our house and she was livid, she was so upset all she wanted to do was go home. We told her that she wasn't staying at her home that night and she would be staying at our house she asked me to take her to her house so she could get some things.
As we pulled up she went into the house and all his clothes had gone apart from his dirt washing, all his trophy's for darts and pool were still on the shelf in the dining room, in a fit of rage Carole started to trash the house and smash his things up, the phone rang and it was your mum I told her that grandma was just trashing the house and she said ok.
After a while the anger subsided and the hurt started to show even moor we got her home and had asked jean and Keith to come to our house (these were carols friends who they had known for years,

Understandably grandma Carole was upset, after a few large brandies Jean and Keith came around and with drinks in hand tried in vain to come to terms with what had happened, grandma wanted to go upstairs to see you and I followed her up stairs to your room where you were fast asleep.
Carole still very upset told me that it would be best if she killed her self, I took the opportunity of us being alone and out of earshot of Jean and Keith and Mandy. I told her how fucking selfish she was and how did she expect me to tell he beautiful granddaughter that her grandma had committed suicide over a selfish bastard who though he was a gigolo. I told her

Not to be so fucking self centred to say good night to you and to get her arse down stairs and pull her self together, I also told her that this conversation was between just the two of us.

When we got downstairs into the lounge your mum, Jean and Keith were sat there looking mesmerised. I looked at your mum and asked what was wrong your mum looked to the side of the lounge door and then back at me. WHAT I said it was then I realised that the private conversation I had just had with Grandma Carole had been over heard by your mum and Jean and Keith on the baby monitor. Every body found it quite amusing.
After that Saturday the name had stuck and from now on we referred to them as gigolo Jack and the mattress, your mum and me had persuaded grandma to do the opposite of what gigolo jack would expect of her and we made her see sense and go to a solicitor and file for divorce.

This she did and it wiped the smile off his face. By now I had found a profound hatred and dislike for the overweight sly bastard who had preached to me years before about the right and wrong about marriage and for the past few years had been having a torrid affair with Margaret the Mattress, she happened to be 10 years younger than grandma Carole but looked 30 years older she had a distinctively hard look to her face, you know the look, the ones cheep hookers have when they think that plying there trade is an art. She had an old fashioned look about her along with the scruffy tainted image that followed her around. From the roomers that preceded her name she would sleep with anything that would sleep with her, apparently she would spend a lot of time at Bredbury hall, a night and country club in Stockport, apparently renowned for whores hanging out there and a pick up joint for sad old fuckers that were past there shelf life, you never know Colette probably frequents that place a lot.

I told Grandma Carole that karma exists and one day he would get his comeuppance.
Your mum and me helped Grandma find a new house and spent what seamed like and eternity clearing over 30 years of hoarded things from the old house. And moving her into the new house. If I remember correctly I took 3 vanloads of crap to the tip, but I suppose that after 30 years of being in 1 place you collect crap.

By the end of the November I had managed to build up the business and now had 30 gardens and was enjoying every minute of being self employed

I had managed to keep a lid on the nightmare that kept raising its ugly head and sending me spiralling into the depths of depression and for once in a long time felt that I had conquered the demon and all would now be o.k.

It was a Tuesday afternoon when I walked into the B&Q store in Ashton under Lyne I had left Steve the guy who worked for me in the van, I only went into the store for a tape measure as I picked up the measure and turned around, I bumped into a guy who abruptly apologised to me. As my eyes met his it was like an atom bomb exploding within my head. A wave of panic flooded my entire body and fear took hold and shook me with all the force it could. I felt the vomit start to rise from the pit of my stomach and his words of "alright mate" echoed around my head, I dropped the tape and ran to the exit, as the damp air engulfed my body the vomit, no longer being able to stay down exited my body 10 years of horrors that had been kept hidden away followed the vomit along with everything else that I had managed to keep hidden away, in the box chained up and hidden away in the darkest part of my mind so as never to resurface its ugly head

I made my way back to the van scared dazed and horrified at the events of the past few minutes, a few minutes that seamed to last for an eternity.
I dropped Steve off at home telling him that I wasn't well and had to go home. By 4pm I was home sat in the conservatory trying to feel safe and trying in vein to sort out what was going on in my head my only companion was a bottle of gin. No matter how much of the gin I drank fear and panic refused to let the pure burning taste of the undiluted gin block out the horror of the bastard who abused me the bastard who earlier today I had once again met and had once again turned my life upside down and inside out.

When Mandy came in around 5.30 it was obvious that I had been drinking but just told her I had to be left alone. The fear and panic of the now un known didn't allow me to sleep every time I closed my eyes I relived the horror of the abuse I was subjected to by my abuser.

It wasn't only the abuse that was now an issue but every other dark secret that I had placed into the box was now out in the open floating above my head ready for the whole world to pick up and look at it and dissect it.
The feeling of pure vulnerability and fear had a grip over my body and even I couldn't start to comprehend a way out of the shit that was going on.

The only thing I knew was that my life was about to change and change in a way that even I could not be prepared for but most of all the feeling of being on a roller coaster that I couldn't get off frightened the fuck out of me, this was a feeling I had no control over and was the most frightening feeling I have ever encountered.
My drinking to blot out the pain continued along with the daily façade of putting on a mask to face the outside world. For the 1st time ever I didn't know who I was.

I am unable to explain how I continued to work and run my business but some how I did. I desperately needed to try and explain and make sence of what was going and to add insult to injury my other dark secret was now foremost in my head.

Desperately confused and trying to keep a grip on reality and normality what ever the hell that was, I turned to the internet in search of answers to the horrors that bombarded my mind through the day and deprived me from sleep every night.

I managed to find a chat room and started talking to people about "me" and about all of the shit that was swimming around in my head. Most of the people I chatted to were as fucked up as me and wernt interested one little bit in the shit I was going through. Each and every one of them had there own problems and moved from person to person using them as sounding boards.

I started talking to a guy called Stephen Noble who like me had his own issues in life, over the next few months I would log on line and chat away this was so easy, I didn't know this guy from Adam and he didn't know me but most of all I didn't have to look at this guy face to face and this way he couldn't judge me, jump to any conclusions and worse of all categorise me.

From the September when my horrors began, through to the following march I muddled through life and the 6/7 months disappeared into oblivion. I have very little recognition of these months, even Christmas came and went and Stephen had become my lifeline.
We had progressed from chatting on line to sending lengthy e-mails where both of us used the other to try and sort out the mountain of shit that each of us had, shit that had now become our lives. Eventually the e-mails turned to letters being written and as Stephen moved around the country our letters and e-mails and our chats on line continued.
Forefront in my mind was not only living with the abuse but also once again having to relive it along with and the hidden secret I have kept locked away in my mind from being 5 years old

Like I have said right from the very start of the book I have known from around the age of 5 years old that I was different and all the way through childhood into adolescence and into adult hood I knew I was odd, different and un like any body else I knew, but after the events of 6/7 months ago I knew exactly what was wrong with me and knew for the 1st time in my life that the feelings and thoughts that bombarded my head wouldn't go away and would only get stronger like they have done over the years and wouldn't go away ever.

Now I had to face all the deamons that were once kept so tightly locked away in the box in the depths of my mind

Tony Standring who I had grown up with, like some friends, you lose touch with them and then get back acquainted with them again. Tony had been working on and off for me some time, he now lives in West Yorkshire with his wife and familey, I adored Tony and his wife Adele the kind of Friends you don't have to say week-in week-out
I got a call from Adele who asked me how I was, Dell had been talking to Tony and he had voiced his opinion how depressed I was at the time; in the conversation Adele asked had I been abused as a child. The words echoed round my head, all I thought was thas if she knows so does everyone else.
I cut short the conversation dismissed her Comments and put the phone down and panicked I now knew I had to tell Mandy and in true PJ fashion I put it down on paper put into an envelope and wrote on the front of the envelope that if she read its contents she could not ask

me how to deal with her emotions and how to cope. I said to Mandy that she should read its contents I gave her the letter and went to the Working men's Club, I had now confided in mandy and given her the gist of what the hell was going on I intended to drink as much as possible to help numb the pain, as much alcohol as it took to make me feel better around 12.30 I tried as Best and as quiet as possible to return the house open the door as quiet as I could, well the quiter I tried to be I think the moor noise I made it must of sounded likie a party of hippoes walking through the door I walked in and half-expected to find my bags packed Mandy screaming and shouting at me telling me to get out. As i reached the kitchen door I could hear Mandy coming down the stairs. With my sunglasses on as to avoid all eye contact your mum came into the kitchen she went to put the light on No! Don't do that I said keep it off I didn't want your mum to look at me I was ashamed, ashamed of me and of what had happened to me, your mum said nothing but put her arms around me held me tight and hugged me, the tears started to flow, tears and then un- controllable sobbing I was totally mentally and physically fucked but Mandy just carried on holding me, we talked for what seemed like hours and hours and eventually went to bed.

As the weekend approached I was at my lowest ebb ever and once again my mind toyed with suicide after all it can be worse and what I was living now and know one would have really missed me or given a shit or even bothered that I wasn't around. but most of all my darkest secrets would go to the grave with me and therefore I can never be judged on most of all can be hated being by anybody beyond belief. for some reason I could not go through with another attempted suicide for it to gowrong like the previous times and then feel even moor of a failour

I had found the number of a help line that I had been looking at it for some time I gave them a call I told the guy on the end of the phone that I need to talk to somebody and that if didn't I would be dead at the end of the week, he took my number and said some body would call me back within then hour true to his word I received a call less than an hour later

Your number has been given to me are you free to talk she said, her voice was soft , gentle and not at all patronising , I pulled up at the side of the road got out so my conversation couldn't be heard and said yes I said that I had a head full of issues and needed to talk to somebody her words were calming and put me at ease she told me she had an appointment for me at 5.30 on Monday and was that ok? That's fine I replied i was given the address of the Manchester office and she hung up.

Again my head was full of mixed emotions, what the hell had I done, there is no way on gods earth that I could sit and tell somebody my deepest thoughts let alone what the hell had happened to me they would think I was a lier, that I had made it all up, she would probably look at me and think ey up another fucked up muppet looking for as bit of sympathy. then on the other hand there was somthing in her voice that made me think that she was genuine, and after all she didn't know me , didn't have my address if I didn't like the outcome I could just fuck off !!

I Finished work on the Monday afternoon around 3, I went home washed, changed and got the train in to Manchester, As the train pulled to a stop at Manchester Piccadilly my head hurt my heart thumped, I made my way to oxford Rd via Deansgate, the quickest route would have been down canal street but that wasn't an option.

I found a bar on Oxford road and made my way inside, I needed a drink, I needed some dutch courage something to help numb the horrors that were on the tip of my tongue something to help me cope, Something to help me tell a totals stranger the shit that was in my head and spiriling out of control, the horrors that had now escaped from there box and free for the world to take a look at my most deepest thoughts.

5 to 5 and trying to look as "normal" and as inconspicuous as possible I made my way towards the door of the big grey building.
With sun glasses still in place (I actually think by now they were glued to my head as I rarely took them off not even inside the house) I rang the bell and waited uncomfortable for the door to open.
A guy appeared at the door and I mumbled that I had an appointment with sue, he smiled and let me in , he told me to take a seat and sue would be with me shortly, by this time the sweat on my palms was beginning to drip from the ends of my fingers, my heart was thumping so fast that I thought it was going to jump out of my chest, the noise of people in another part of the building took my concentration and added to the fear, people laughing and shouting, my concentration was broken by the familier voice from the phone "Hello" she said "you must be Phil", I nodded nervously, " would you like to follow".
She introduced herself. "My Name is Sue Duncan Gilbert" she said confidently, Her curly hair and large round glasses complimented her looks and he smile was soothing, caring and I suppose a little sympathetic, after a few formalitles on how the session would run she asked me to explain what was bothering me.

It came from no where! Everything that was now out of the box swimming above my head exploded like an express train, the words pouring from my mouth at break neck speed telling her all the shit and thoughts that had haunted me for years and years and years,
The shit I had so carfully locked away and hidden from the world, as the 50 minute session came to an end the darkest and most well hidden secret I had evey kept tripped of my tongue and for the first time in my life not only had I admitted to myself but I had admitted it to a total stranger.
For the first time in 35 yrs I told her what had bothered me from being 5 years old, not only did I have all these issues that I had just told you but also that I am Gay. Not only Gay but Gay and married, and not only Gay and married but Gay, Married and I have a daughter.

I waited for her reaction for her to fall about in fits of hysterics to fill the air and the building with laughter, for her to judge and ridicule Me! ……..But it didn't happen.
Her once again calming mood and sense of care filled the room her compassion seamed to envelope me and all the shit I had just thrown at her didn't seam to faze her in the slightest .
It was agreed that I would return the following week and we would start to look at the issues I had one by one, As our conversation came to a close the panic started to fill the pit of my stomach I now had to leave the "sanctuary" of this safe place and get back into the stream of "normal" everyday people on Oxford Road without anybody seeing me leave the building, with the sunglasses fixed in place I left by the door I came in by and in no time at all I was back in the flow of people going about there every day business, The commuters making there way home, people running for busses and trains and each of then un aware of the fact that I had just unloaded 35 years of shit on to somebody else's shoulders, told them my most darkest and intimate secrets and admitted to not only a stranger but to my self that I was a Gay man.

OH FUCK!!!!! What have I done?

When I got home your mum asked me how I had got on, as far as I knew your mum thought I was being counselled for the abuse, little did I know that the letter I had given your mum, she had like any other desperate person looking for the answers to why her marriage was failing had read between the lines and even though not confirmed by myself in person knew what the score was.

I knew by now that the closest friends I had, the people and friends who had always been there for me through thick and thin had a right to know about me.
My head is strange and a jumble of a million and one pieces of shit swimming around and I am unable to concentrate on work, I called up to Hall and Ogden waste paper merchants in Ashton under lyne it was owned by Lynn and Graham Hall, Lynn's husband a recently passed away and Lynn had continued to run the business with her son, Lynn was and still is another of my close friends even though I had known Lynn and Graham since being a child, since grahams passing we had become close friends, I can honestly say that in the 40 years of being on this planet Lynn is one of the very few people who dose not judge any single person in any way shape or form, she accepts every single person she meets as an individual regardless of there colour creed or sexuality and I now needed a friend to talk to. To off load some of my emotional baggage, to try to make sense of the life I had that was spiralling rapidly out of control and moving to a dangerous level.

I walked into the yard and as always it was full of activity, bails of paper being moved and loaded on to wagons and the general comings and goings of a busy working company, Lynn's son Allen acknowledged me as I crossed the yard and entered the office
I was always greeted with a kiss on the cheek and a hug from Lynn and today was no exception, the only difference was that today I was moor emotional than usual and had to battle hard to avoid the tears flowing, as I was handed my coffee we chatted generally about work and life, I spent the next 20 to 30 minutes scooting around the houses trying in vain to muster up the courage to tell Lynn I was gay.
I could hide my emotions no longer and the tears started to flow, as I told her I was gay her reply was …And…. So what! you are you you are the most individual you there is ,you are unique! The hugs that followed made me feel secure for the first time in a long time, in a strange sort of way this made me accept myself even more.

I knew as I left the office Lynn wouldn't be on the phone telling all and sundry about my life Lynn along with Sue ,Stephen and Gill were the only people I could trust, really trust, on my way out of the yard I bumped in to Vijay, Vijay and his family owned a local garage and carried out all the repairs and work to Hall and Ogden's wagons, Vijay like Lynn always met you with a smile a warm and compassionate smile and it was followed with a friendly handshake.

I had known for sometime that Lynn and Vijay had been seeing each other and trying there hardest to keep it under wraps, Lynn had confirmed my suspicions in our conversation. I couldn't judge either of them and being honest I had noticed just how happy Lynn had seamed over the recent months, Vijay makes her happy makes her smile makes her realise that there was still a life out there for her after the passing of Graham. Vijay and I passed a few pleasantries and I once again was on my way.

As the weekend approached I met up with Gill and invited both her and Fred over on the Saturday night for a meal and a few drinks.

These were regular nights where we would catch up with the comings and goings of each others lives and enjoy each others company along with good food and drink,

Gill and Fred were accustomed to the coming and goings of the spirits that frequented the house and took it as part and parcel of life at Number 52, they were used to the footsteps you heard on the floorboards up above and even being passed on the stairs by something that wasn't there.

You were fast asleep in your bed and Mandy and Fred were in the conservatory chatting I stood at the back door with Gill whilst we had a cig, having always felt comfortable in Gills company I told her that I was seeing a councillor and that I was Gay, she took it in her stride like I knew she would and like Lynn the few days previous didn't judge me or pass comment and didn't lecture me, this was when I started to relise who my true friends really were.

On the following Monday I called in to see Gill for a reaction to my recent revelation, she had been un fazed by what I had told her and most of all not shocked or repulsed, we spoke for hours ironing out the myths and general chatting.

Gill mentioned that she wanted to go to collage to do a counciling course to enhance her position at work she asked me if I fancied doing the course with her, I agreed and later that week we made our way to the collage to enrol on the course

Walking back through the doors of a school environment instantly took me back to my childhood, the familiar smells of cleaning fluid, disinfectant, Floor polish and new paint, the smell of authority and above all the smell of the abuse I had suffered as a child.

In my heart I knew that I was dealing with these emotions as an adult but I also found it so difficult because deep inside there was still a little boy wanting to run away, ther little boy who wasn't in control and wasn't in charge of the situation, the little boy who knew the other side of school life. A side of life that no child no matter how old or from what back ground they came from should ever have to contemplate let alone endure, survive its horrors and then some years later have to re-live it again.

Pulling myself together Gill by my side we aproached the doors of the collage.

The fear and panic rose from the soles of my feet. this was the first time I had been in a school environment as a pupil since I was 16 years old, an environment I had spent years trying to get away from. Even when I had to go to parent's night to see your teachers it took me all the strength and courage I could muster up to get through the door, because every time I step through that school door I relive the horror of my childhood.

We received the forms and sat down to fill them in within minutes we were in fits of giggles partly from nerves and partly from me giving Gill the raised eyebrow look, a purely innocent look that I had mastered that would reduce Gill to a fit of giggles followed by another look of amazement as if I didn't have the slightest idea of what she was laughing at.

We left the collage to wait the 2 weeks until the course started.

Over the next few months my counselling with Sue continued and I slowly started to make sense of what was going on in my head and the confusion that had dominated my life. It wasn't as if there was just 1 issue to confront but a whole lifetime of them.

Along with my counselling sessions I started with my counselling course with Gill and the freaky fuckers who attended the course, hand on heart I think that me and Gill and 1 other person were the only sane ones there,

There was a lady who attended the course who loved the sound of her own voice and enjoyed making sure she took centre stage, but 99% of the time it had nothing to do with the course but some sad freaky church group she attended called cell, basically a group of brainwashed fucked up do Gooding interfering nobody's who popped around to other interfering nobody's houses and chatted about shit.

One night just as our break had started I was chatting to our tutor about dreams and did she ever remember her dreams and most of all did any of them ever come true. On the return from our break I was set on by the freaky bitch from cell and another god bothering woman, a school teacher, who I had taken instant dislike to for obvious reasons, she had befriended by the cell woman and told me what a disgrace I was meddling in voodoo and witchcraft,
I was astounded that first she had been listening to our conversation and secondly she had the nerve to think that remembering dreams or even talking about them was voodoo, I kept me mouth shut and knew I would get my own back.

Taking into consideration we were in an environment where as a group we had made a pact that we would not judge I was gob smacked that she had broken this rule, later that evening towards the end of the lesson she was once again on her soap box and this time telling the group that she had been discussing one of her 1 2 1 sessions with another group member with her husband and how he had commented on what a lovely person this other pupil sounded and she might also be a wonderful person to join cell. This was now taking the piss and I wasn't happy at all she had no right to discuss anything that was said within these four walls with any body outside. I know others felt the same about this betrayal.
I continued to give Gill my raised eyebrow looks and turn her from a sensible 40 something year old into a giggling wreck to the surprise of the rest of the group and follow it up with the look of surprise wondering what she was laughing at.

My e-mails and letters continued to Stephen who had become a close friend and my personal councillor and in return I had started to council him to help him deal with his own feeling and thoughts and the fact that he was a gay guy,
The friendship that was forming between Stephen and me was unexplainable.
I had come to the conclusion that the moor people I talked to the moor sense I managed to make of what was going on in my head,
I had been chatting to another guy called Chris for a while, Chris lived alone and was very self centred and quite selfish in his own way, but I believe that this came from his childhood. He lived in Ipswich, a place I had heard of but only on a Saturday afternoon as a child when mum sat in the kitchen doing the football pools.

Chris was totally the opposite of Stephen, Chris was self centred but he was a good listener and able to throw a different angle on some of the shit in my head. Having been talking to Chris for around 6 months I decided to go down to Ipswich to see him.
Me going away for the weekend was partly me doing my run away from the problem act, you know! if I go away from the problem I don't have to deal with it, what I didn't realise being the stupid bastard that I was, was when you run away you take the problems with you, they only go away when you deal with them.
I made my way down to Ipswich on the Saturday morning, I had booked into a travel lodge in the centre. My first impressions was how flat the area was I was used to seeing the pennies and hills and stuff but there was nothing but flat ground.
I met chris later that afternoon and it was good to put a face to the guy I had been chatting with for the past few months, we spent hours talking about our own problems and issues the following day I got the train back home.
I got the train at Ipswich station and had a 20 minute journey before I had to make a change.
I stood on the platform on that damp September evening recollecting my visit with Chris and going over in detail the conversations we had had.
I shared the platform with 2 back packer and my thoughts.

As the train pulled into the station and stopped I boarded the train and made my way to the first class carriage I have always had high standards and openly admit that I am a good natured snob, I upgraded my ticket from second class to a first class ticket and took my seat by the window , the carriage was empty apart from me, as the train started to pull out of the station a coloured lady in a blue two piece suit entered the carrage and made her way towards me she stopped at my table and announced that she would take a seat opposite me, she stowed her case and took a seat.
She introduced her self telling me that her name was Mrs Clarke, I told her that I was Phil and that I had just been to see a friend in Ipswich for the weekend.
Out of the blue she asked me why I felt that I had the right to stop my mum seeing my daughter, and she said that the argument was between your mum and me. Basically the argument consisted of my mother having very little to do with you, even though we lived about a 5 minute walk from her house she very very rarely came to see you,

she had all the time in the world for Colette's son. And Anne's kids but very little for you, but both me and your mum knew why, it was basically due to the fact that both anne and Colette Needed mum and used her for a free baby sitting service and anything else they could get out of her, where me and your mum had always been independent, from the day you were born we had made sure we had a child minder in place because we both had to work , we didn't need my mother to run our lives and I think that she didn't like it

I was astounded by the depth of the knowledge Mrs Clarke had about me and my family but in a very strange way it didn't faze me, I wasn't frightened or worried it just somehow felt right and my conversation continued with Mrs Clarke for the 5 hour Journey into Manchester. As the train pulled up into Manchester Piccadilly I offered to take Mrs Clarkes case from the train I thanked her for her wisdom and for allowing me to see certain situations from another angle, I set her case down on the platform and her your voice in the distance shouting Daddy.I watched as you ran towards me with the wonderful words of daddy ringing in my ears, I turned to say good by to mrs Clarke but she was no ware to be seen.
My puzzled look gave your mum the opportunity to question my amazement on my face. She asked me who I was looking for and I told her about Mrs Clarke and the 5 hour conversation we had had and the fact that I had placed her case on the platform,
With a confused look your mum told me that I was the only person who got out of the 1st class carriage, NO!! I proclaimed! I sat and chatted to Mrs Clarke and I took her case off the train, once again she told me that I got off the train alone, Even more confused I once again proclaimed that she got off the train with me . it was then that you spoke up and described Mrs Clarke to a tea, right down to the 2 piece suit she was wearing and the suitcase she carried, See I said to your mum she did exist I wasn't going mad but to this day you mum was and still is very adamant that I left the train alone.

Now going back a little way when the lady who served the beverages on the train came through the carriage I got a coffee and asked Mrs Clarke did she want a drink but in a polite manor she refused my offer. Now thinking back to the lady with the drinks trolley, she didn't acknowledge Mrs Clarke in the slightest, so was I sat talking to Mrs Clarke? (in my eyes yes I was) but did the lady with the trolley think I was talking to the chair in front of me like one of the many nutters that ride the network rail system every day of the week that she must see on a daily basis, but you Laura just like me did see Mrs Clarke and it wasn't a figment of my imagination.

She may have been my gurdain angel or a spirit guide but to this day Mrs Clarke made me realise that as a parent I don't have the right to make decisions that will affect you and you will make up your own mind regardless.

September of 1997 and my brother was getting married, Pete and Joanne had been together for about 7 years, I honestly liked Joanne but she was a moody bitch and would often speak for Pete, now this pissed me off, on occasions when they came to our house you would offer him a drink and she would pipe up no thanks he's fine?

He had arranged his stag night and we went on a pub-crawl. It was around 3 in the morning when we eventually got a taxi. The driver asked us had we heard about princess Diana and dodi alfyrd, we thought it was a joke and awaited for the punch line, but the driver was disgruntled and couldn't wait to get us to our destination. As got in the house I put the TV on and instantly started to sober up.

Princess Diana and her lover dodi alfyrd had been killed in a car accident. I couldn't believe what I was watching, Royalty doesn't die. This wasn't happening; I shouted your mum and we watched together as the drama of a royal death unfolded. I felt numb and dumb struck. I eventually went to bed and on waking the next morning thought I had dreamt the images that had disturbed my drunken slumber, on putting on the t v I again relived the images from the night before and reality hit home.

The events of the next week were bizarre, like I said, in my life time no member of the royal family had died and especially some one likes Diana, who was nicknamed the peoples princess.

It was touch and go weather Pete's wedding went ahead or not and on the Saturday afternoon he married Joanne. I still have the wonderful picture of you and me that was taken that day; you were dressed in a gorgeous orange dress and new shoes and looked the angelic angel that you were.

The following week and the world stopped to morn our princess as she was laid to rest.

For some unknown reason my correspondence with Stephen had come to an abrupt end and my letters and e-mails were not being returned, my last e-mail and letter had been sent a few months ago and to date I had not received a reply, I was now worried and once again sent an e mail to Stephen. I asked him to let me know that he was ok and safe

I few days later I received an e mail from him that just said I need some space but please don't go away. All I could do was wait and bide my time

I had begun to rely on my sometimes daily correspondence with Stephen to help me get through the confusion that had now become my life, but my head was now in bits half of me thought that I had exhausted our friendship with the constant demands I was making on him in the desperate attempt to sort out my life but the other half of me know that something much deeper was going on and until he was ready to confide in me there was little I could do, my hands were tide but in true fashion I continued to e mail Stephen daily letting him know that I was there for him, the only difference was that I know felt very alone.

My councelling sessions with Sue continued and I was finding it increasingly harder to delve in the horrors of my past to dissect its contents look at them and then place them neatly back in the box knowing that if they ever escaped again I had delt with them , they could no longer hurt me and I could place them away instead of them sending my life spiriling into depression with a bottle of gin for comfort.

My Monday sessions with Sue started with me finishing work around 2 pm, going home and getting changed and then getting the train in to Manchester, I still couldn't face my sessions without a drink inside me and my sunglasses fixed firmly on my face, as I have always said the eyes are the window to the soul and your eyes tell everything about a person.

I knew by now my life was changing and changing rapidly and at great speed and that my life with you and your mum was never going to be the same. I still put the mask on every morning to leave the house and face the world and this had become a ritual every day, the hardest part was keeping it in place and never allowing it to slip.

I wasn't ready to change and be the real me yet as my head still had so many emotions to deal with ,as I have said before when ever I went into Manchester i would never enter the village or walk down canal street, I avoided the village like the plague and supposed I did this because if I acknowledged this I would be admitting to myself that I was gay and at this stage in my life this was something that only myself, Stephen, Sue, Gill and Lynn knew and sometimes even that felt like to many people.

On one of my Mondays I got off the train around 3.30 at Piccadilly and made my way towards Canal Street, my heart was thumping and with sun glasses in place I started to walk through the village my eyes taking inn every bar, table and person I passed taking every conceivable step to look " Normal", about a qtr of the way down canal street I was approached by a woman who asked me for a light for her cigerette I fumbled around my jeans pocket for my lighter clumsily dropping it on the floor I picked it up and gave her a light and a deep voice replied ta love, I was mesmerised at her appearance over 6 foot tall in an ill fitting wig and clothes that didn't fit right. To my horror I then realised that this woman was a man in drag, He looked like his wife had popped out to bingo and as she got out of the door he had run upstairs thrown on some of her clothes and a wig and painted his face with her make up the lipstick looked like it had been applied with a 4 inch paint brush and finished off with a moth eaten fake fur coat. She totted of in high heals leaving me stood alone in canal street physically disturbed.

Was this was the gay scene was all about? As I got to the end of Canal Street I checked the time I had over an hour to kill before my session with Sue and as always alcohol beckoned.

On the corner of canal street was a pub. I went through the door and ordered a pint from the bar I knew it was a gay pub but also knew that I needed a drink, just when it seamed that I was starting to make sense of my life my head once again became confused and muddled and for the first time in my life I was stood in a gay pub feeling very venerable, scared and confused. To be honest it was just like any other pub I had ever been in and its clientele like in any other I has seen, it was what you would call a well used pub and the carpet on the floor was matted with spilt drinks and burnt cigarettes like most pubs it had the aroma of stale beer and the occasional whiff of toilet blocks from the urinals in the nearby toilets, as I started to relax a little I began to look at the other people in the pub not one of them looking gay ,

When I was growing up the only gay role models I knew were the likes of dick emery, John Inman and Larry Grayson but none of the pubs cliental even slightly resembled the camp TV personalities that I had grown up watching on TV, I stood at the bar making no contact or conversation with any body else, just letting the alchol relax me I left

the pub, hopefully unnoticed and slipped back into the main stream of city life making my way to my session with Sue.
Once inside my session with sunglasses in place I continued to tell sue about the deamons that stopped me from being happy in life and that stopped me from being the person I really was.
Every time sue had approached the subject of the abuse I would instantly change the subject I wasn't prepaired to go through that again , it had happened to me once and I didn't want to have to re live those feelings again, to me it was unthinkable. Sue's approach to my demons was remarkable and for the first time in years, like a child I let down the barriers that had been locked in place for years and the horrors of the abuse came to the forefront of my mind and tripped of my tongue with unbelievable ease, through the tears and uncontrollable sobbing I relived each and every day he raped me. Mentally physically and sexually along with the mental torture that I endured along the way, as I looked at Sue she was crying and visible upset. This wasn't supposed to happen! Why was she crying? I now felt guilty that one of the only people who was helping me to sort out the shit had been reduced to tears, the emotions that I was going through were to be honest unbelievable, emotions that I had never felt before, I had always been so careful to conceal my emotions and feelings, hiding behind my mask and keeping it in place, as the 50 minute session came to an end, I left totally drained very confused and hurt. Hurt because the person who was helping me and 1 of the few people I had let in to my fucked up world had been reduced to tears

On reflection my counselling was going well and I had managed to arrange my work schedule around my sessions, I always made sure that I was in Manchester no later that 4 pm as my sessions were now 5.30 pm this gave me the opportunity of going for a few drinks before hand. For the much needed Dutch courage I needed to face my fears. I could now walk down Canal Street feeling fairly confident but still never made any eye contact or conversation with anybody.
I could even walk into the sticky floor pub (the new union) order a drink and stand in the same spot I always felt comfortable, a spot at the bar by the door, this being my escape plan should I feel the need to run away.

It was on this particular Monday afternoon that whilst stood at the bar this guy came into the bar and ordered a pint, I had noticed him on several occasions over the past few weeks, coming in at the same time obviously on his way home from work. He looked like a decent guy short hair around 6 foot in height and what looked like a decent toned body, on every previous occasions he had always stood a good 10 foot away but I had always noticed that when I did glance a look his way he would be looking at me and when we both made eye contact we both very embarrassed looked away.

Today was different he got his pint and sat right opposite me, after around 10 minutes he approached the bar and asked me to keep an eye on his pint whilst he went to the loo, "sure" I said, he went to the loo returned and drained his glass and ordered him self another pint. We started to make general chit chat and I noticed the time, I made my excuses of having a meeting at 5.30, as I got to the door he asked me if I fancied meeting him for a drink on Friday evening, sure I replied . I will meet you in hear at 8 he said. I left and made my way to my session with sue.

Each and every session I had with sue became easier and I knew that I was turning a corner I could now look at the issues that we were dealing with and put them back into the box.

For the first time I felt that the abuse that had happened to me seamed a very distant memory, it also seamed to have happened to some body else weather this was the way that I coped with it, the way that I dealt with it, it now didn't seam to matter or hurt as much as it had done in the past. Even dads death and all the emotions that came with it seamed a long time ago and that they didn't hurt any more.

It was in this session that we were talking about coming out as a gay person and all the emotions that you go through, Sue was telling me that she knew just how I felt as she had also gone through similar experiences when she came out..

My mind flipped a double summersault, what did she just say? Stop rewind!! I could not get my head around what she had just said to me she was gay?????? this just proved how bloody nieave I really was, since I started going into the sticky floor pub I had seen builders, doctors, labourers, policemen, solicitors, and office workers who were all gay this proved to me that you didn't have to ware a dress and run around singing tunes made famous by Judy garland to be gay.

But most of all that I was just like every one of them "normal" and as Lynn and Gill had pointed out I am the most unique individual me that there was and there was no other me in the world.

As Friday approached I had mixed emotions of meeting this guy, the main reason was that I was still married to your mum and no matter how you wrapped it up it felt like the gay me was going out on a date.

I told you mum I was going out with some friends from the counciling session, what you have to understand laura is that at this present time in my life I am two separate people I don't want you to think that this is a cop out or an excuse but this is the truth and just how it was.

I was Phil married to your mum with you as my gorgeous daughter and then there was the other Phil, The gay guy who was starting to accept him for the person he was.

I put on a pair of jeans a t shirt and jacket and made my way into Manchester As I approached Canal Street my heart was racing and confusion was paramount in my already screwed up head,
I couldn't believe how many different people there were on the street, laughing and chatting with some wearing the most outrageous clothes I had ever seen, There were good looking guys wearing nothing but a G string and leaving nothing to the imagination, guys openly kissing each other in the street and guys holding hands, Jesus Christ I thought! What the fuck have I just walked into, this isn't the canal street I had known at 5 oclock in the after noon. The canal street that I had become comfortable with, this was a total different ball game. This was like a fucking freak show! a total nightmare! It was bizarre, was this how I was going to have to live my life from now on?

I made my way down Canal Street and into the sticky floor pub the hustle and bustle of the hundreds of people all out enjoying themselves frightened the hell out of me, constantly aware that I was being stared at, being watched and looked at by complete strangers. This was the first time in months that I didn't have my trusty sunglasses on and felt totally naked but most of all very vulnerable and very insecure.

As I walked through the door of the sticky floor pub it resembled nothing of the pub that I knew or that I was used to, to start the place was absolutely hammered wall to wall with people and had more characters than the fucking Jungle book.

I made my way to the bar and managed to get to the place at the bar where I felt safe and was used to standing. It was five minutes to eight as i ordered my first pint; The guy behind the bar took my order and asked how I was. It was the same guy that served me on a Monday before my sessions with Sue, as strange as it sounded he was a friendly face in a very large crowd and all the confusion that went with it. As I stood at the bar taking in all the comings and goings I was keeping an eye on the clock it was five past eight and still no sign of the guy I was supposed to meet.

As I waited feeling like a fish out of water a guy at the right hand side of me started to talk to me he was in his late 50s farley over weight and a piece of hair dragged over his head from one side to the other, " "can I buy you a drink" he said "no thanks" I replied "I am waiting for somebody", he continued to pass half hearted compliments and try to engage me in conversation I just wished the floor would open up and swallow me or that at least a bus would have driven through the front of the pub and taken out the fat bastard who was now starting to piss me off beyond belief.

He then told me he was a clairvoyant and that I had lovely hands and could he read my palm I told him I worked for the vice squad and thought that he should fuck off before I had him arrested, next thing he was gone and once again I was left alone.

I drained the contents of my glass and glanced at the time it was just gone twenty passed 8 and I was ready to leave when he walked through the door. Sorry I am late but the bus was late…. Bus I thought I don't do busses they in my eyes quite common, have you never heard of a taxi I thought but hey at least he eventually turned up.

I must admit the he had the most gorgeous eyes, I started chatting to him and my insecurities came to the forefront I told him that he really didn't want to get to know me as I was one fucked up guy who carried so much baggage. I was gay I was gay and married I was gay married with a daughter and I had so much emotional baggage to top it off, he just smiled at me and so did his eyes. We continued chatting about things in general and about what work we did. After a few drinks he said shall we go into Via Fossa, I agreed but deep down I was panicking I was now leaving my comfort zone and going into another bar, a bar I didn't know with people I was not use to, I had only just got used to being in the sticky floor pub but now I was doing a fucking pub crawl up canal street with a gay guy I didn't know

Via fosse was what I would call normal I suppose, a 50 50 mix of both gay and straight people men, women couples ect but most of all I was still having a problem getting my head around 2 guys openly kissing each other in a bar and not a single person battering a bloody eyelid. This was alien to me and totally the opposite to the way I had been brought up . I was mesmerised as to how many gay people there were all in one place I suppose that the only conciliation really was that for years I had thought I was the only gay person in the world.

I still felt nervous about the new surroundings I was in even with my new friend at my side, as 11 30 aproached we made our way on to canal street and stood against the wall continuing to chat and to take in all the sights that the village had to offer.
I had just put out my cigarette out when what happened next turned my whole life upside down, back to front and inside out. He placed his hand on the back of my head and pulled me towards him he then kissed me , don't ask me why but I responded and kissed him back , then all hell seam to let loose in my head . WHAT THE FUCK AM I DOING??? Kissing a fucking guy in the middle of Canal Street in front of hundreds of people.

I stood there totally motionless as life carried on regardless of what had just happened. What the fuck had just happened and most of all why the hell had I just kissed him back, he smiled at me and told me to relax. And that it was no big deal. To him it was obviously an every day occurrence but to me it was far from normal.
My head was awash with a mix of emotions and feelings that I had never felt before , yes it was normal and yes it did feel right but it still felt wrong! but most of all did any body see me any body I knew.

By 2 am I was very drunk and sat in his flat a very scruffy 1 bed council flat in a tower block in the middle of Salford, I vaguely remember getting into the taxi to get there but the rest is a blur, now I was sat in his flat still drinking and listening to music from the 80's he sat next to me and once again we kissed he smiled at me and asked me to come to bed with him. Instantly sober and well out of my comfort zone I panicked like I had never felt before and the panic I felt battered the life out of my body, I needed to run and get out of the situation I was in, I didn't want to be hear and couldn't cope with what he had just asked me I declined and made my excuses and left.

He must have thought I was the freek from hell and most of all a complete twat, Around 4am I was home and feeling worse for ware just when I thought I couldn't get any moor confused, just when I thought I was starting to get my life in order something like this comes along and throws me back into a state of confusion.
I now knew exactly who and what I was but was so unsure how I proceeded from hear.

 I was still chatting away on the chat line to any body that would listen to me basically , for a while I had been chatting to a guy called John he was a married guy with a family who lived in Leeds I still felt that even though I had Sue to sort out my emotional state I needed an outlet and a person to talk to, even though I continued to send my regular e-mails to Stephen I still got very few e mails back and the e mails I did get back made no sense, there was something going on that I didn't know about something that I had no control over, all his e-mails ever asked me to do was to bare with him.

I met John one Saturday afternoon at Piccadilly station a 40 + year old guy who over a period of time helped me so much he helped me become the person I am today and I hope in time I will once again meet up with him face to face so I can thank him personally I owe him a lot.

Eventually after months of nothing I received an e mail from Stephen, very brief and to the point, hello he said how are you, my reply was instant am fine but moor to the point how are you where have you been and more to the point are you ok,
I had for months had a very strange gut feeling that something wasn't right but for the life of me I couldn't put my finger on it and after all this time with no, or very little contact to receive his e mail was like all my Christmases coming at once. My life fell to pieces at the words I was reading, my body shook and my head couldn't take in what I was reading. Stephens sister Jo had been murdered by her boyfriend and

left alone to die he sent his mother to the flat with her baby daughter Daisy to find Jo.
Not only had Stephen been coming to terms with coming out as a gay guy he now had to deal with the emotions of grief.
The feeling of guilt and the enormous amount of sadness I felt shook my body, I had never felt this amount of sadness in my life, this guy had been forced to sink to the depths of despair the lowest point that any human being could ever have to go to and I wasn't there for him, a few days later I received the news paper cuttings from Stephen regarding Jo's death and the trial, looking at the cuttings in my hand I felt totally fucking numb my brain refused to take in what I was reading this murdering evil fucking bastard was little moor than scum and a prison sentence was to good for him, Not only hade he taken J'os life but the despicable piecs of shit had ruined so many others in the process ,to start with there was daisy, she would grow up with out a mum never knowing personally the loving caring person who brought her into the world.
Then there was Stephen a loving caring brother who's life had been ripped apart at the seems having his sister, best friend an confident taken away, Stephens mum and dad loose a daughter, Gran, cousins and close friends lose there loved one and then indirectly there is me, I know I have no right to tag myself on to the end of the line but indirectly this has now effectd me it affects me because it has affected Stephen
I knew I shouldn't judge this guy as I dont have the right, but to me the most important thing was Stephen, this was a guy who had helped me so much and I was now feeling his pain, it made the shit I had been going through over the previous months seam like a jubilee party this was serious shit but the worst of it was that I was unable to take his pain and grief away, I was unable to help him like he had helped me. I knew there was no instant fix to this but I was adamant that I would never not be there for him again.
Over the following months our friendship grew stronger and stronger and indirectly started the process of becoming each others councillors helping the other dissect and unfold all the memories and confusion that freely swam around in our heads.
Eventually we were back on track and a day didn't go by without a letter or an e-mail being sent or received.
I filled Stephen in with what I had been up to over the past months and in true Stephen style not an ounce of judgement was passed or a derogatory comment made.

My sister Anne had spent months picking up the pieces of her life, and eventually had a new man in her life, she was now moving with her new man and family down to Wales to start there new life together. Ann and James were having a farewell meal for the family and close friends in a local pub / restaurant a week or so before this myself and Anne had a conversation about me and my new friend "IT", Anne being the outspoken person she is asked me straight out was I gay and was "IT" my partner, yes I said . I knew that it wouldn't belong before the bongo drums would start banging and all and sundry would know my secret.
Even though I was now coming to terms with my new life as a gay guy I was still very uncomfortable and it was taking a lot of getting used to. I still worried what every body would think and worried about how many of my friends I would loose. In the conversation with Ann I told her that she should not tell anybody especially my sister Colette.

As you may have now gathered I have a very distinctive dislike for Colette and this was my life and it had nothing to do with her. Within less than 12 hours Anne had had a conversation with both peter and Kathy and mum had overheard their conversation. On the day of the meal we arrived at the pub and my family met "it" for the first time, every body in the restaurant apart from Colette new that "it" was my partner, they sat Colette and me at either end of the table of 20 as Anne knew that had we been sat in spitting distance I would have ripped her head off her shoulders. Whilst having the meal people were asking about the new house and when we were having in ect, I enjoyed this conversation as Colette wasn't receiving any attention what so ever. Colette approached me and said "what's all this nonsense about "it" being your partner and that your gay" I told her that he was my partner and that I was gay I then shouted over to mum and said will you explain to Colette that "it" was my partner and that I was gay" mum turned to Colette and said " oh yea it's true , I just haven't had time to tell you, Not one single person around the table battered an eye lid. Colette looked at every single face and waited for there reaction but it didn't happen, rather perturbed and annoyed at being the only person not to know she turned to me and said "oh" I don't mind I have gay friends and and and anyway I am bisexual myself. Anne overheard her statement and like me we both burst in to fits of giggles.

Just as I had predicted 2 days earlier she would try and turn the situation to make sure that she had the attention, my reply was simple. "Fuck me! I can't even be fucking gay without you jumping on the bandwagon. Basically it backfired on her and she just made herself out to be the pathetic dim-witted Muppet that we all know she really is.

By now most of my closest friends and my family knew I was gay and knew the situation I was in and the life I was now leading. One day I got a text from Brenda asking me if I wanted to go out for a drink and a chat, she told me that we could go somewhere where people didn't know me if I wanted. I hadn't got around to telling Baz and Brenda yet but realised from the text that she obviously knew but it just needed confirming. I knew Brenda would be fine but had my doubts about baz, to be honest and fair I had nothing in common with baz what so ever. Baz lived and breathed football and football was something I detested with vengeance, I would rather have my arms and legs ripped of by a rabid pit bull terrier than have to watch a football match let alone have to play the blessed game. I wondered how the conversation would go, but agreed to going out for a few drinks.
I knocked on the door and baz opened the door, he still had his slippers on and I knew straight away that he wasn't coming out for a drink with us. I was relieved as I now didn't have to cope or deal with the awkward silences that there would have been.
Bren was ready and we started to walk into Denton, I told her that I was gay and that "it" was my partner, she told me that she had put two and two together and come up with 4, I asked did baz know and bren laughed, she said they had been discussing it a few days previously and when she mentioned to baz that she thought I might be gay he paid me the best compliment I think I have ever received.
He said that he always knew that I was "different" because I didn't like football. This made me laugh out loud, it was a priceless fantastic statement, bren told me that as baz had known me for years he accepted me for me and regardless of my sexuality it didn't matter. She told me that baz didn't know any body that was gay and it was an alien concept for him, this I could understand as I still was getting use to me being gay.

December 1999.

In the many attempts over the past 18 months to find out who I really was and find the real me I , in my wisdom had spent quiet a time running away from the situations that I didn't want to address and this was no different from the many other times. I went away at the beginning of December to New York, then onto Texas and on to Chicago. It was my first holiday to the states and went with Chris my mate from Ipswich, I flew down to Heathrow from Manchester where I met Chris then the following morning we flew direct to New York. I knew that by now my life had changed dramatically and it was still changing at a phenomenal pace, I also knew that my life as a married guy was coming to an end. Slowly over the past few months I had been detaching myself from your mum and the life I had as a married man. I knew that if any one of the 3 of us had any chance of happiness I had to leave and live my new life as me.
Gill had now become a key role in my life at this point, not only was she my friend but she had also become my best critic, the 12 weeeks we had spent on our counceling course had indeed moved me further along the path to finding and accepting the real me .

The counceling course had certainly been an eye opener, I can honestly say that for the first time in my life I had actually met the biggest bunch of freaky fucked up individually I had ever met in my life, each one of them with there own issues weather it be wanting a carrear move or wanting to just go on a course because as they were on beniffit they could get it for free or to try and drum up business for the freaky fucked up church group called cell with the obnoxious woman who's husband had the imprint of a stearing wheel on his chest. This just proved that I wasn't the only person who was running away in life regardless of the reason.
I had managed to conquor the fear of being in a school enviroment but this had also allowed me to realise that when you sit in a one to one counceling session you actually step in to that persons shoes and for the 50 minute duration of the session you live there life and when that person hurts you feel the hurt as well.
This now explained why some months previous when I was in a session with sue, she ended up in tears, it wasn't the fact that I had hurt her but the fact that she stepped into my life and she felt my pain.

The Christmas of 1999 was like any other Christmas, the only good thing about it was I had you my gorgeous daughter and your mum in my life, but only I knew that things were changing fast and I wasn't sure how long if ever that would last for, I must admit that I did enjoy spoiling you beyond belief and that wasn't through guilt but pure unconditional love.
We had been invited to Tony and Adel's house for New Years Eve they lived in a small picture post card village called Lluddendon foot in west Yorkshire.

When we arrived the close had been transformed into a Christmas picture post card they were celebrating new years eve in style, Tony's house was a three story house with the garage under the house, the residents of the close had turned garages into a bar, an area for food and areas to dance. The street was decked with bunting and lights adorned the garages even some of the Christmas trees from lounges had been brought in to the street. The place looked amazing. As always the welcome was warm and friendly and the company second to none.
As midnight approached you had been unable to keep your eyes open and had gone to bed you were fast asleep and blissfully unaware of the pending festivities and the arrival of the year 2000.
As the clock-hit midnight one of Tony's neighbours was letting off some fireworks, you know the ones that give a quick fizz and bellows of smoke. I grabbed Tony and took him to the car, your mum and I had bought some very large fireworks, and in the true drunken stupor we decided to let them off. Regardless of having to stand 25 metres away we let them of to the gasps and joyous applause of the onlookers how the hell we didn't end up with third degree burns, and minus a few fingers I will never know. All in knew was that we were letting the year 2000 in with style.

My first recollection was of being in a very clinical and unfamiliar place, with the surroundings and noises that UN nerved me. I was sat on a bed surrounded by a curtain, I got off the bed with the fear of panic rising in my body(this was a feeling that I had become accustomed to over the years) but this feeling was stranger the rest. I moved off the bed and saw your mum sat on a chair at the side "where am I " I demanded to know "where you were, your mum told me that I had had an accident and you were safe asleep at Tony's, fear took over my body as I was unable to grasp my surroundings, where am I, I screamed, I wasn't in control of this situation and didn't like the feelings that accompanied the feeling of mass confusion that had now taken over the whole of my body.

Your mum told me that I had been in an accident and I was in Halifax general hospital, she told me that Tony had fallen on me as I was going into the house and he was coming out of the house , that I had hit my head on the cobbled path and stopped breathing, she told me that I had a very nasty gash to the back of my head "don't you remember" she asked, utter confusion had gripped my body and the fear of not remembering sent waves of panic through my head as I sat there on the edge of the bed, what Mandy was now telling me resembled exactly a dream that I had had just over 12 months ago. The dream I had was so vivid that when I woke up I wrote it down , it had been so life like that it had played on my mind for quite a few weeks after.

In the dream I remember a person lying on a cobbled path with blood pouring from a wound to the back of the head there were lots of people standing around the person on the floor Tony and Adele were stood at the feet of the guy on the floor and your mum was knelt by his side, there were other people crowed around the person on the floor but I could not see there faces, nor did I know who they were, the guy on the floor wasn't breathing and a lady was giving mouth to mouth, due to the location of the accident they were unable to send a traditional ambulance and a medical range rover along with a doctor was dispatched to the accident scene , the next recollection of the dream was the person who had the accident was sat on some stairs bleeding heavily from the head, when the doctor arrived to access the situation your mum was asking the person who had had the accident did they need to go to hospital to the amazement of the onlookers your mum was telling the onlookers that he had previously seen the accident in a dream, the paramedic had a flashing Christmas Santa

pinned to his top pocket the dream ended with the person being taken to hospital.
Like I said the dream was so vivid that it had prayed on my mind for quite a few months and always stayed in the back of my mind.

I needed to get out of the hospital and get out now! I needed to make sense of the confusion that pounded my head but most of all needed to see you and make sure you were fine.

The events of the dream and the flashbacks of the accident and the past few hours had great similarities.
I sat in the back of the taxi with your mum my head bandaged up to fuck and with the mother of all headaches. Reality hit home, as I recalled the dream and once again told mandy what had happened in it she told me that the events of the accident were identical to the dream I had had. We arrived at Tony's and Adel's house and all I wanted to do was go home, I didn't want to sleep and didn't want to remember the dream or the accident, I was now so fucking confused, there was no difference in the accident or the dream and they had now merged into one, your mum told me that as she had had a drink she was unable to drive home yet and we should go to sleep, the relief of seeing you fast asleep and totally oblivious to the events of the past evening gave me some much needed comfort but didn't ease the confusion that continued to batter my brain.

Little by little over the next few hours the events of the accident came back to me and it dawned on me that the dream I had experienced some 12 months previous had been a premonition right down to the flashing Santa on the top pocket of the paramedic.
On our return home I looked at the dream I had written down some 12 months previous and event after event image for image word for word it was identical to the accident I had just had.
This had now freaked the hell out of me, later that day I called Tony to apologise for ruining there night, adele told me that it wasn't a problem she also told me that after my accident whilst I was at the hospital Tony had fallen in the garage and a trip to casualty had revelied a couple of broken ribs.

Well like I said I was letting in the year 2000 with a bang and in true style I think I just managed it …..

My friendship with Gill, had, like Stephens become a lifeline and just for the record at no point in all of this did Gill just ever take my side of the situation, on many occasions she gave me a fucking hard time and always made sure that I looked at the whole story, including your mums and yours,

I knew by now that I was preparing to leave you and your mum but with gills and Stephens help I had to be sure that the impact on both of your lives was as easy as possible.
I knew that the impact of me walking out of the door was going to have a devastating effect on all three of us, (You have to remember that I still loved your mum so very very much the only difference was is that I wasn't in love with her and believe me Laura their is a bloody big difference,) I knew that life as we all knew it would never ever be the same again

I also knew that I had to absorb as much of the pain and the hurt as possible and try so hard to not make your mum hurt, be assured that I was and still am so very aware that your mum did get hurt, felt betrayed and felt cheated but the hurt and betrayal that your mum felt was far less than what she had of felt had I been a complete bastard . No words will ever be able to explain how much shit and pain I absorbed to enable you both to be able to come out the other side of this and still feel that you have a life and to come out the other side relatively unscathed.

The only people closest to me to to help me make my decision but in no way influence it were Gill and Stephen and for this I will be eternally grateful to them both.

On my return from America it was at this stage that we had moved from Booth Street and moved into grandma carols house Booth Street had been sold and the furniture put into storage.
Grandma carol knew that things between your mum and me were not good but did not know the extent of what had happened over the past 12 months. My counselling session with sue were coming to an end and I had eventually accepted me for the person I was, like I have said I knew that I was leaving and that there was never going to be a good time to do it.
My relationship with the guy I met in the sticky floor pub was progressing even though I knew deep down that it was far from right.

Your mum and me were house hunting and found a house in Nelson Street in Hyde the property had recently been completely renovated and after our first viewing it was perfect for you I pointed out at this stage that I would move in but I would not be staying for ever
Your mum asked me to tell you that I was going to leave and asked me to make sure I left it until after your birthday.

On the Sunday morning as like most of the others I was going to the tip to empty the weeks rubbish from the van, and like so many times you came with me.
As you sat in the van I started to drive up Dowson road in Hyde I told you that mummy and daddy hadn't been getting on for sum time and in a few weeks time daddy wasn't going to be living with Laura and mummy I tried so hard to emphasise to you that it wasn't your fault and that I still did and always would love you and that you would still see me, as I glanced over to you as you sat in the passenger street I watched as the tears started to stream down your tiny face, you told me that you weren't crying but your eyes were just leaking a little bit.
 I felt such a bastard, worse than I had ever felt in my life , I felt that I had shattered your life and dreams and blown to pieces the foundations of your whole world in one small sentence.

I was now totally convinced I had fucked your life up completely. I remember having to pull up at the side of the road as my own tears and the wave of emotions surging through my body stopped me from seeing and being able to continue to drive , I moved from the driving seet and sat next to you in the middle seat of the van where we both hugged each other and cried endlessly.
I repeatedly over and over again told you how sorry I was trying so hard to try and fix the life I had just shattered and at the same time trying to ease the enormous amount of guilt that I felt. As we hugged I didn't want to let you go, in my mind I thought that if I stopped hugging you the second I stopped would be the second I lost you forever and the thought of that was unbearable. As the tears subsided we continued to drive to the tip.

I do hope that you believe me When I say this, but until the day you die you will never know how bad I felt about the conversation I had just had with you but I also knew that there was no other option and what I was doing was best all round.

I moved out of nelson street on Saturday afternoon April 13th 2000 and moved in with "it" my new home was a fucking tatty high rise council flat in the middle of Salford, when I got to the flat he was lay on the bed pissed out of his tiny mind and the only words he managed to utter was "oh so you left em did you"

Mr recent fears of moving into his tatty hovel of a home had been confirmed and I knew that I had made one of the biggest mistakes of my life but I also knew that it was a mistake I had to make to enable me to become completely the real and honest me.
I also knew that I wasn't going to spend the remainder of my time in a shitty run down squalid Salford flat so I started to immediately look for somewhere for us to move to.

Over the next few months I got to know the real "it" a selfish self-centred, lying, lazy, abusive pathetic violent alcoholic, who was so insecure and jealous it was unbelievable, I had never in my life come across such a twat of a person but stupidly believed that if I took him out of the situation and into a knew life he would change.

Having spent more than enough time in his shitty dump of a home I eventually found a new home for us to move into. We bought a new 2 bed house just outside Manchester and with a lot of get up and go we eventually moved into our new home.
I furnished the house from top to bottom and the only contribution from "it" was his kettle and his double bed.
We had been living in the house for around a months when he stopped going to work telling me that he was depressed and needed time off work to get better, I would work a 14 hour day come home from work cook a meal and he would still be in bed pissed out of his brains .

Like I said previous, he was very jealous and the first time you came to stay he was his usual drunken self.
I knew that I had to be on the ball and also knew that he could flip at any time. I had cooked dinner and you helped me wash and dry the dishes you politely asked him if he wanted to play monopoly with you and you were met with a mouthful of verbal abuse, delicately I decided that the best course of action was to put you to bed. I tucked you up read you a story when I went downstairs he had been to the shop for

more alcohol and was well into his next bottle of hock wine.(cheep shit that council scum drink)

He sat in his piss-stained jeans and started to complain how I spent too much time with you and I should take you back to that whore of a mother you have. I was livid but my only concern was that you were upstairs and I had to get you out and make sure you were safe.

I went upstairs and told you to get dressed I had to lie to you and tell you that "it" was upset as he had received some bad news and I was going to take you to your mums. You got dressed and came down stairs and said thank you to him and I opened the door of the van as I was putting your seat belt on he stood at the door shouting obscenities and I then snapped.

I turned to face this pathetic mess of a thing propped up at the door and flew at him like a bull in a china shop my hand fitted comfortable under his throat as I pushed him through the lounge and into the kitchen where I wedged his head under the hood of the extractor fan above the hob his eyes bulging wide through the lack of air getting to his lungs.

I told him how horrified I was that he was jealous of a 8 year old child and had the mordacity to call your mum names, I continued to tell him that I was fed up with his laziness and drinking and being the totally bone idle bastard that he was as I left the house, I shut the door that hard that the frame moved and twisted rendering the door un-open able as I drove towards your mums the anger inside me was bubbling and had I returned that evening I would have openly killed the scummy bastard.

I knew by now that he was never going to change and that in his eyes I was a soft touch and was there to keep him in the alcohol that he desperately needed to get him though the day. What he hadn't banked on was that I also had a temper and the behaviour if "it" over the past few month had pushed me beyond the point of know return where I had snapped, justice was the look of horror and surprise on his face as he realised what was happening and that I wasn't going to be walked over.

I spent the next few days staying at you and your mum's house and calming down, as for "it" I wasn't a bit bothered about him. After a few days I received a call from him apologising profusely about his behaviour telling me that he will change and would I come back home. I agreed to come back home on the condition that he went back to

work and started pulling his weight around the house, I also told him he needed to sort out his drinking, he agreed.
I went home and the house looked like a squat, the sink was full of dirty pots and the rest of the house looked like a heard of fucking tramps had moved in I spent the remainder of the day cleaning the house , I wasn't used to living in a shit hole and I was adamant that he was not going to turn it into a replica of the shitty high rise council hovel he was used to living in. when he got home he told me he had been to work but I had my doubts, he smelt like a brewery and something that the cat had shit on and looked dreadful .

I said nothing about the state of the house and he said nothing about how clean the house had become since he left it.

Over the next few weeks things didn't change one little bit in fact they got worse he continued not to go to work and his drinking spiralled out of control, I started to find hidden empty bottles all around the house, hidden even in the oven and washing machine.
I remember going to bed 1 night at around 10.30 and was rudely awakened at ten past 2 by the thudding and blaring music coming from downstairs, I went down and demanded to know what the fuck he was playing at. "Just listening to music" he said what I replied at full fucking volume he smiled and I realised he was now playing mind games, not only was he jealous of Laura and Mandy but of me.

He was jealous that I ran my own business and that I had standards and morals what had he actually got. Being honest nothing!! he was a lazy idle alki who was living in a new two bedroom property and out of his comfort zone, he wasn't used to living in a nice house with nice things around him he was used to living in squalor in a shitty rough high rise hovel in Salford, the penny had just dropped I now realised that you cant take the council out of some people and once scum always scum, before you think I am judging well I am not, I am not saying that all people who live in a council house are scum what I am saying is that "it" gave people in council houses the bad name and the stigma that goes with it. "it" was scum, the lowest of the low and whilst I am on my soap box the sex was absolutely awful it was like having sex with a sack of spuds, emotionless and not at all exciting but most of all loveless. He was incapable of loving anybody except himself and the next bottle of cheep shitty hock that he constantly poured down his throat.

Two days later and the final straw, having been at work since 6 am I got home to find the house again looking like a replica of steptoes yard I put dinner in the oven and went upstairs to clean the bath that looked like a pig had been rolling about in it, well it wouldn't have been him as his personal hygiene matched the squalor he was used to, I heard him fall through the door and then barge upstairs, obviously blind drunk and for what ever reason in a foul mood. He stumbled up the stairs cursing and blinding on how I had made him buy this house and how he missed his gorgeous flat, I couldn't believe what I was hearing, how can you compare a first class hovel of a flat to a privately owned house, I told him that I wasn't prepared to put up with a any moor and I was leaving, it was like lighting the blue touch paper he started to kick and punch me and threw mw down the stairs as I started to get to my feet I saw he had been in the kitchen and had a knife in his hand he was that drunk and capable of anything and I knew I had to get out, as he lunged for me with the knife I rolled out of the way and he fell to the floor I stood up at the same time as he did and head butted him right on the nose as he fell to the floor I made my way to the patio doors making sure that I locked it behind me I got to the van jumped in and started the engine my heart was racing and blood pouring from cuts to my face and eye.

As reality kicked in the tears started to fall I couldn't see where I was going , I was just driving and didn't have a clue where I was driving to. My concentration was broken by the ringing of the phone "hello" I said, the friendly voice of your mum on the end of the phone made me try so hard not to allow her to sense that something was wrong, but your mum being your mum couldn't be fobbed off.

He's done it again she said, when are you going to wake up and stop it happening. Come hear and stay in the spare room for a while, I was homeless in a strange sort of a way and that fucking scummy bastard was living in the lap of luxury
I needed to clean myself up and couldn't let your mum see me in this mess, I told your mum I didn't know where I was, she asked me what landmarks I could see, just then on the left hand side I passed housing units of hollingwood "oh bloody hell I thought I always wondered where that place was, your on Oldham road she said and directed me to the motorway, I was still covered in blood and most of all my pride was very badly damaged, I had tried to prove that I could

make it work and failed miserably , on my way to your mums I had to call at Lynn and Vijay's as I needed to get cleaned up, Lynn and Vijay as always made me feel so welcome and helped me understand that things were not ment to be and no matter how hard I tried it wouldn't work and I had to accept that.

When I got to your mums the only clothes I had were the ones I stood up in after she ran me a bath she nipped out to a
Asda and bought me some work socks and boxer shorts and t shirts. This made me feel so humble and in a way upset me that I had actually left your mum but she still had the heart not to turn her back on me.
It was at this point that I decided that I would never return to "it" and as for the house I didn't give a shit about it I needed to detach myself from "it" and the house, I started by informing the utilities companies, and the poll tax that I no longer lived at the house and the bill liabilities were "its" responsibility
I then contacted the Halifax who the mortgage was with and informed them that the relationship had broken down and that having been thrown out of my home I was no longer in a position to pay the mortgage and that I suggest they reposes the house as there was equity in the property they were happy to allow no mortgage payments to be made and for "it" to continue to wallow in self pity

You will have noticed that all the way through I haven't mentioned his name and have referred to him in the latter stages as "IT" the reason for this is that I believe that for a person like him to treat another human being in such a disrespectful way and with such contempt and deceit is far from right, if I had deserved the treatment then I could hold my hands up and say yep I was in the wrong but my only crime was to give him my love and respect and try to offer him a better life, from the day I left his name has not passed my lips and until the day I die I never will. As far as I am concerned he was a part of my past that had to happen for me to get to where I need to be.   And in my eyes it's his loss.

From the September when I left until the Christmas I was plagued by text messages and depending on what state of consciousness he was in depended on the context of the text message. On one occasion I received a phone call from the control room of the 999 emergency services, "IT" had called 999 and asked them, as he had no credit on his phone to contact me and ask me to bring him cigarettes as he had run out. I openly denied all knowledge of knowing him and realised he would stop at nothing to get what he wanted in life even if it meant putting other peoples lives at risk.

I received a call from his boss one day asking me why he wasn't in work, I told him that I no longer had anything to do with "IT" and I wasn't bothered if he was in work or not, to be honest I wasn't bothered if he was alive or dead, if he was dead at least the house would have been paid for but I suppose it wasn't meant to be.
A few days after the call from the 999 controll room I got a text message from "it" to say that he had taken an overdose and didn't want to live any more(well at least we were thinking on the same lines now) I called to the house which now resembled a scene from a local authority tip, the kitchen looked like a fucking bomb had dropped he had even been sick in the sink that was full of dirty plates and cups, the toilet was covered in dried shit and the carpets (less than 12 months old) looked like they had been down for years there were empty cans and bottles strewn around the house and the bed was like a stinking piss and shit covered mess in the corner , the stench in the house was absolutely diabolical and then there was "it" un shaven un washed and looking like a corpse………..mmmmmmm I thought looking nearer to death than I expected ….there may be a god after all.

He thanked me for coming over and asked me for some money , fuck off I thought!! Had you not had enough from me .He told me that he had taken an overdose of the antidepressant tablets he had been prescribed so I called an ambulance and they admitted him to North Manchester general hospital, I told the doctor that he had taken an overdose and had further tablets in his pocket to take another overdose later, I suggested they section him under the mental health act as he was a danger to himself and others and they agreed and sectioned him for 21 days this gave me the opportunity of cleaning the house from top to bottom after all I still had a vested interest in the house and it needed to be sold. "It" was mortified at being sectioned but I did it for the right reasons after all the shit he gave me I still cared for him in a bizarre sort of way.

7 months after leaving "it" I was still living at yours and your mums house I had just had a reading from a clairvoyant she had told me to a

tea the events of the past 12 months along with the new home that I was going to be moving into, she told me that I would be moving into Mossley, a place that was near enough for me to sort me life out but far enough away so that people wouldn't bother me. In early March I had eventually managed to pick the pieces of my life up and I eventually felt ready to move on again, your mum and you had been fantastic, my online and letter writing friendship with Stephen continued to go from strength to strength and gill continued to emotionally support me and keep me on the straight and narrow. I had been home hunting for a few weeks and I had managed to find a 2 story flat in top Mossley that was for rent I had about 3 weeks before I moved in and over the past few months I had been buying bits and pieces for my new life and my new home.

It was around this time that I got a text from Stephen telling me he had changed his name to Will.
Wow!!! Hang about I thought Name change how the hell could I automatically just start calling Stephen, Will,? And why had he changed his name from Stephen a few letters and txt messages managed to clarify the situation. Stephen had always been known to family and friends as Will but used his first name Stephen on legal documents ect, to him it was normal to change his name to will.
To think that I had first got to know him by his internet name " Foxy boy 69" then Stephen and now will, but I took it all in my stride.

At the end of a day its only a name and after all he was one of my closest friends and a guy who I owed my life to.

Having eventually got "it" out of my system I needed to get my life back on track totally, that meant that as a guy with a high sex drive I needed a sex life. I decided to go on a chat line and after all it was only sex.
Before you sit and frown at what your reading at the end of the day it was just sex I was not the first and definitely wont be the last to use a chat line to meet another person for sex. I was a grown man knew about safe sex so don't look at this with disgust, like I said it's me being honest.

I went on to the chat line one evening and got talking to a guy,he described himself as a cute Anglo Indian guy we exchanged a few

messages on line and he asked me where I was I told him I was in Hyde town centre and he asked me if I wanted to meet him that night. You bet I replied, not trying to sound to desperate lol.
We met on the town hall steps in Hyde (yea I know such a cliché) and he looked like a really nice guy
It was such a nice feeling being close to another person knowing that what I was doing wasn't wrong or dirty. Like I said it was just sex between to consenting adults. I must admit that the sex was good. very good and the first time I had had sex in the back of a car in a very dimly lit car park lol,
He told me his name was J and he gave me his number. I went back to your house feeling like a teenager, this was the first time in years that I felt happy, but with the thought of "it" still in my mind I new I had to be cautious .

The next day I was frantic, I had somehow managed to loose j's phone number from the previous evening. I had no way of contacting him didn't know where he lived , Basically new nothing about him apart from if I was being honest I liked him.
My flat in Mossley was eventually ready for me to move into, your mum had been shopping with me to get my T.V, video, cd player microwave, washing machine, and bedroom furniture over the past few months i had picked up lots of things as I needed to start again, having furnished 1 house and being left with nothing I had no option to start again, I signed the lease on the flat and got the keys, it was a 2 bedroom flat on 2 floors you entered off the street and went up the first flight of stairs to the large kitchen dining room and large lounge, you went along a corridor and up the next flight of stairs to 2 bedrooms and the bathroom.
I loved the flat; it was my own home with my own possessions and my own company. I had room for you to come and stay and now I was able to do what I wanted. The only downside to the flat was the smell of grease from the café downstairs next door but one and the old fucker who lived in the flat next door, when he started coughing the walls shook, but apart from the two minor problems I loved it.
I had been in the flat about a week when I went back onto the chat line after a few minutes I got a message, it was from j asking me how I was and why I hadn't been in touch , my heart missed a few beats as I told him I had lost his number I gave him my number and told him to call me. He did and we spoke for what seamed ages, I told him I had now moved into the flat and that he should call up.

Over the next few weeks J became a regular visitor and I was falling for him hook line and sinker, when we started seeing each other it was agreed that it was just some no strings fun but you cant help the way you feel. We went into Manchester one night and to be honest it was the first time I had been in Manchester for over 12 months, even though I was now comfortable with my sexuality and happy with me I still didn't do the gay scene very well I still found the gay scene a bit sleazy and like a meat market. I have always had a problem with people staring at me but when in the village that's what people do they stare and look at you.

Whilst in Manchester we had a fantastic night we had been for a meal and then onto canal street and into some of the bars and then we went into Essential night club three floors of gay people enjoying a Saturday night out, the music was fantastic.
On the ground floor they played the latest dance music and state of the art laser lights mesmerised me as they moved to the beat of the music, I looked on at all the people 99% of them gay all enjoying themselves. The top floor played music from the 80's and I stood speechless as I watched the obvious usual crowd carry out all the actions to the music that was being played, every one of them in time and not one of them missing a single action, stood on the stage for the world to see, , I have to admit it was a little bazaar to watch them

I left my drink with J and went to find the toilets, somehow some ware I got lost within the club and couldn't find J. something in my head kicked in and I knew I had to get outside the club. There was only one way in and one way out and something my dad had told me many many years ago came back to me if he went in the doors he would have to come out of them and I should stay put and wait for him to come out.
I made my way outside and sat on a bollard outside the club watching every person come out and go in I couldn't believe that I couldn't find him in the club but there were so many people on the 3 floors, I stood for over 40 minutes when all of a sudden j came out of the club he ran over to me and threw his arms around me he held me tight and hugged me 2 "I thought I had lost you" he said, I told him I could not find him so I sat outside and waited for him to come out. He then told me that he was falling for me. The words echoed in my head and I felt I was on cloud nine, I had fallen for j by the second time I had met him

and to hear him tell me he had fallen for me was the best feeling I had had in a long time

I woke early the next morning and spent a good 30 minutes watching J sleep by my side, watching him breath watching the look on his face and wondering what he was thinking. It was a wonderful feeling waking up next to a person I felt comfortable with. Over the next week or so j would call in on his way home from work or from the gym and occasionally stay the night.
It was on one of theses nights when J called in after the gym, I made dinner and we went to bed, whilst in bed J said that he had something to tell me, he told me that he was a trainer for a bank and the bank he worked for was the Halifax. I sat bolt up right with my head swimming with confusion Oh my god I kept repeating. From the day I had met J I had told him about my life and "it" I had been bleating on for weeks on how I was writing to the Halifax to ask them to repossess the house and all along he worked for them he told me he would help me write the letters to the correct people and hopefully we would get somewhere. Whilst all this was going on we were blissfully unaware that the local co-op was ablaze it was only when I went to the front door to say good by to j that we noticed that the whole co-op had gone up in smoke.

Eventually after 8 months I got a text message from it. He had decided that we should put the house on then market; I could not believe what I was reading I sent him a text and told him I would contact an agent. As soon as I sent the text message I contacted Bridgefords estate agent and explained the situation, they were going to send a somebody the next day . I text him back and told him to make sure that the place was tidy he replied and said o.k,
I hated being nice to him but if it finalised the last piece of the jigsaw I would do what ever (well within fucking reason).

The next 8 weeks seamed like hell having to be extra nice to the piece of shit that made my life so bad, all I wanted was the house to be sold, I got a call from the agent and we had been made an offer I sent him a message and told him that it could be complete within 2 weeks if "it" agreed. He agreed to the price and eventually the house was sold. I came out with around £5,000 this was nothing compared to the amount the lying bastard had managed to wangle out of me the only

good thing that would come out of it was the hope that he would spend his money on drink and kill his bloody self.
After the house was sold I received a letter from "it" and felt that I needed total closures from him and wrote him a letter back . this was the letter I wrote him.

Dear "IT,"

Thank you for your letter. It seams to have taken forever to sell the house but at last it has all gone through.
I can only speak for myself but the past 19 months have certainly been a learning experience.
I have looked back over this time and only now realised that for whatever reason it was all ment to be, and was part of the overall masterplan called life.
When I moved in with you on the 13th of April the decision I had made was not an easy one to make but I decide to give up everything I had worked for and all the security I had to live with you.
From day 1 I gave 110% to the relationship and wanted so much to make it work. you didn't even give 1%. When I moved in on that day you were pissed out of your skull lying in bed, that should have said everything. All you could see was your next shag and a meal ticket moving in, you must have thought that all your fucking Christmases had come at once

When we bought hacking street I envisaged I happy life with my partner, at no time did I ever expect to be treated like you treated me. For the 19 months I have known you every day you abused me in some way shape or form. (I know you don't like me using the word abuse as this becomes reality.)But that is exactly what it is.
Weather it was name calling, public embarrassment or humiliation or physical or verbal abuse, I realised that the only reason you wanted to stay with me was not because you loved me for the person I was but for what I could give you and what you could get out of me. You treated me like a cash card ! and your personal taxi service
You knew I was a hard worker and you knew I could earn money by the work I did. You spent 19 months taking from me with no intention of paying back a single penny and abusing my trust to your own gain to feed you drinking binges and to abuse me as you thought fit, if you didn't get what you wanted or if things hadn't gone your way at work

and things didn't go to your plan "it" would have a tantrum I would be abused a little more from you And you would make up another story or event to get sympathy or attention.

What you didn't understand was that you didn't have to do this as you had my attention and my love, in the first 8 months we were together you spent this time seeing how far you could push me, even when we moved to our new home you continued on your selfish I man reigeme of abuse and bullying and for what?

At the end of it all you lost the lot, just as myself and so many others told you you would , you lost your job, you lost the best person to have walked into your life to be your partner, you lost your self respect and eventually lost your home,

I worked so hard to make sure we had a very nice home, we had money to go out and that we could go away, but all the time you kept chipping away at the love and respect I had for you until there was nothing left.

You asked me so many times why I came back to you at Chrismas? To be honest I felt sorry for you and I pittied you, basically that was all. I tried to kid myself that I still loved you but being truthfully honest I didn't, by this time you had managed to kill off any love I had for you or any chance of me ever loving you again I had also lost all the respect I had for you, how can you respect a person who has done so many nasty, vile, and evil things to you

In your letter you say that you are sorry for all the nasty things you have done to me.
This I can believe, but not for the fact that your sorry because you loved and lost me but due to the fact that you lost your second bank balance , someone to bail you out of the constant shit you produced , someone to run around after you, someone for you to abuse and publicly humiliate

You actually made me believe that you tried to kill yourself to get me to come back to you. You watched me as I made an idiot out of myself as I tried to get help for you and all the time you were laughing at me behind my back, that was pathetic. you havnt got the guts to kill yourself, your too much of a coward and far to selfish, Oh and for the record it was me that convinced the doctors to section you , it wasn't hard but I was hoping that once they sectioned you they actually might keep you locked up for ever.

You tried to make me believe that Lloyd at your place of work actually abused you , when all along it was you who was doing all the abusing. But being as calculated as you are you even you couldn't pull that one off to your satisfaction and in the end you were sacked.. To put the record straight neither myself Mark or Kevin or Andrew ever believed Lloyd was to blame, but they wont admit this to you , LIKE YOU THEY ARE COWARDS and just a few of a long line of people you call friends but are just past shags and the people you use on a regular basis.

In the 19 months I was with you, I became isolated from my family, my friends ,I lost my home and I lost the person I loved and respected, I was left homeless and with a debt of around £7,000 all because you were a very selfish very calculated, lying cheating abusive person. I would hate to have to go to sleep with your conscenence ....or lack of it.

Thank you for your concerns regarding my happiness but it need not worry you in the slightest.

After you threw me out of my home, that was the final straw , it took me until just after the Christmas to pick myself up dust myself off and get my life back on track, you see even you couldn't keep me down I just become a hell of a lot stronger.

In the past year, my life is as I want it to be.

 I have a wonderful partner who is genuine, honest careing and loving , he treats me like a human being and loves me for the person I am and not the person he wants to change me into. He dosnt treat me like a meal ticket or a private taxi.or a shag, and oh" just for the record he is very good in bed not some motionless pieces of loveless trash like yourself.
 He isn't a deceitful lying cheat, He accepts I have a past like everyone else dose , he idolises My daughter and gets on with my family , my ex wife and my friends. He makes me laugh But most of all he dosnt abuse me. he is like me he is a very hard worker and he has standards and he has goals in life, he dosnt think the world owes him a living and he is far from lazy he is actually the total opposite of you

we have recently come back from a 2 week holiday in Mexico after moving into our home.

You asked me to find it in my heart to forgive you.

Do you remember , your screaming fit in front of all your work mates at the hotel when you embarrassed and humiliated me.
Do you remember your tantrum on a plane when I paid for you to go away, along with you tantrums in Dublin.
Do you remember how jelous you were if I spoke to another person, my daughter my ex wife my family and friends.even customers
Do you remember calling me every name under the sun you could possible dream up, bastard twat cunt whore rent boy these to mention a few were the politest
Do you remember playing me off against Mark, Kevin and Andrew Jackson,
Do you remember cuningley extracting money from me to feed your drink problem, as you were to idle to go to work?
Do you remember treating me like you personal taxi service?
Do you remember lying to me continually?
Do you remember all the times you distrusted me for no reason..
Do you remember smashing up all my c.ds. and videos because you were having a tantrum like a spoilt little brat
Do you remember screaming abuse at my little girl because you were jelouse of my love for her
Do you remember all the abuse you gave me just for the hell of it.

Unfortunately as forgiving as I am I will never as long as I live be able to forgive you for what you put me through mentally. physically , emotionally and financially.

If you remember I sent you a tape with a song called out of reach by Gabriell it sums up the relationship we had to a tee.

You were incapable of loving me , you used and abused me as a person, you abused my trust and my good nature, I think your incapeable of ever loving any one hence why your over 40 years old and still single with a string of broken relationships ,shags and jobs behind you

I was actually in the process of working with the Halifax to have you removed from the house and the house sold when you agreed to sell the house , 19 months later you are a just a name and a part of my past that I have delt with, You may actually have noticed that I refer top you as "IT" you don't deserve to be called by your name.
I gave you the world and you threw it back in my face with the contempt only you could.
I have spent months having to be nice to you just so the house would go through without a hitch so I could get what is rightfully mine and get you out of my life for good
please don't for 1 minute think I actually care if your well of not, you gave that privalidge away when you threw me out.

Never once since I met you did you ever love me, care for me or respect me,
You only loved how much and what you could get out of me.
At the end of the day real true love only comes into your life very seldom , true love came into your life in the form of me, you chose to throw it away,
I have found happiness and I have never been happier and I accept and I am more than comfortable with me being a gay guy,
I am proud to be the person I am, after all I could be a cold selfish heartless abusive shallow lying cheeting person. (you)... thankfully I am not

As the house is sold we need no longer carry on the charade of being nice for no reason, there will be no need to write again as this will be my last ever letter to you as all future correspondance from you will be put in the bin un opened i am glad In one respect that I met you as it has made me realise that in this world there are some very loving and caring people and on the other hand there is you and people like you ,self centered, shallow , lazy lying cheeting deceitful & underhanded

I am so glad that you have ended up in a tatty council flat in the middle of Salford, along with your tatty furniture and your concenoius and the only friends you will ever have are the string of has been shags that you continuasly sponge off, I hope every day you wake you relive the horror of what you actually did to me (if your ever sober long enough to remember) and I look forward to the day somebody repays you twice fold .and believe me this will happen, I hope every day you look at or use any item I bought for our home your conceounce plays havoc with you, at least you can live off the state claiming benefit and let the decent people of the country keep you in the squalor you are used to , I am only to happy that you had a chance to see how other people live and you have now ended up back in the gutter where you truly belong.

I cant say it was a pleasure knowing you as believe me it wasn't, I actually cant remember any single good time I spent with you and I actually don't know what the hell I ever saw in you , it proves that you cant judge a book by its cover , even sex was a let down like I said it was like shagging a sack of spuds, motenless and dead.

I wont wish you well but in the same sentence I wont wish you any harm either I firmly believe that you will live the rest of your days bumming around from 1 shag to the next, exploiting others as you have exploited me and many before me,
I will take delight in knowing you will never be happy but most of all you will be a very sad very lonely person,

It must be an awful thing to go to bed every night worrying that you might pass away all alone in the night and no one would even miss you or know you were dead for days/ weeks / months? And would any body care…..I think not!

Good by

I never heard from "it" again but I do know that somewhere down the line our paths will once again cross, the difference this time is that I am a hell of a lot stronger and wiser and I will never be put into that emotional situation ever again,

Having read the letter I wrote to him you might think that I was very hard on him and not at all nice. The money the house and the abuse is, in my eyes irrelevant, they were my mistakes and I got hurt for them, the one thing that hurt me more and what I can never forgive myself for was the way he spoke to you and the way I put you in a terrible position, a position of putting you in the same breathing space as that vile abusive piece of shit.
The only good thing is that hopefully you were to young to remember just how vile he was to you. All I can say is I am truly sorry.

I know that my problem is that when I gave anything I give my all and don't keep anything back in case things go wrong

I enjoyed living in the flat and enjoyed the time I spent with Jay, he still stayed at his mums a few nights a week and this didn't bother me as I understand that she is his world, and I suppose that as she has brought him up single handed since the death of his dad it must be hard for him not to see her, he told me a few days ago that he still pays his mum rent of some form or another and the only reason for this is so that he doesn't have to give up his room and that if everything went wrong at least he has a place to stop, I will add at this stage that this doesn't fill me with confidence but its his money and he can do what the hell he likes with it.

My friendship with Gill had become a wonderful friendship; through all what I had been through she had been there through thick and thin and never once judged me,
Every body should have a friend like Gill a genuine person who you can call any time day or night, and throw as much shit at them as humanly possible and not be judged, but to have that friend allow you to see that there are two sides to every story, to allow them to let you see that you are not always right and most of all make you realise that the actions that you take don't just have an impact on your life but the lives of the others around you.

Had Gill not been my friend the actions I had taken and the decisions I made would have impacted your life and the life of your mum and the damage caused would have been catastrophic. Please don't for one minute think that the friendship was all one sided, on many occasions I repaid Gills friendship with my own words of wisdom when times in her life she needed the same friendship and a person to allow her to see things from another angle and of course my wonderful words of advice and wisdom..

The landlords of the flat and the letting agents were what you might call useless, the repairs on the flat would never be completed and the letting agents would just let themselves in as and when they wanted, after one such occasion we changed the locks, Jay came home one day and said he had seen a house on Stockport road that was for let and he thought we should go and take a look,

We made an appointment and on the Saturday morning we went to view the house. As we walked in the lounge was a fantastic size and had the most amazing picture window that looked over rolling hills and fields. The house was on three floors and the kitchen dining room downstairs was as huge as the lounge, another couple were viewing the property at the same time and the guy showing us around the house said that if we wanted the house we would have to get to the letting agents before the other couple, we hastily made our way to the agents and started to fill in the forms for the house 10 minutes later the other couple arrived and informed the agents that they would take the house, you should have seen the look on there faces when they were told that it had already been let to us, she wasn't best pleased but we then found out that she had already missed 2 appointments to view the house , her loss and our gain.

We eventually moved from the flat on Stamford street and into our new home on Stockport road,

After a weekend of moving furniture from the flat to the three-storey house we were eventually all sorted by the Sunday evening. We couldn't understand why our legs hurt so much but soon realised that going up and down stairs as many times as we did had an impact on the old legs.
We also realised that you never went up or down stairs empty handed, you always made sure that if going up 2 flights of stairs you brought everything you needed and vice versa.

The neighbours were what you could say were "odd" the houses on either side were also rented and both couples were very homophobic and colour prejudice. The only nice couple on the row were David and Helen, a young couple who were expecting there first child and a lady called Ann who lived next door but one who was widowed.

We had only been in the house a few weeks when one Monday morning I woke around 5.30am and as I lay in bed I could hear water dripping. I got out of bed and went downstairs, to my horror it was raining very heavy outside and there was water pouring through the windows, it was like there was no glass in the windows as the water poured through.

I went into the kitchen and the same was happening there I went into the rear bedroom and the same was happening there. I spent a complete day running up and down three floors mopping up water and wringing out wet towels.

That evening after getting hold of the landlord they appeared with a couple of small towels and assured us that this happened on the odd occasion, there gesture of a couple of small hand towels made me laugh inside, I had a dozen sheets and towels on radiators drying and the thought of two hand towels was a bloody joke. We were just worried that we were going to get the blame for the place being flooded.

We settled into our new home and aver the next 12 months carried on our life as normal, we would go to work, enjoy our nights out and have some of the most fantastic parties, weather they were house warming, Christmas, birthday or just a general get together

One Sunday evening we were on our way back to the house, we had been to Jays mums for dinner and had also been to the gym. as we were coming up to the harts head pub on Mossley road there was a car about 10 yards in front of as we started to go around the bend a police range rover came hurtling around the corner with lights flashing and sirens sounding, within a split second the range rover lost control and cut between the car in front and our car, I honestly thought that the thing would stop but it smashed through the fence and somersaulted into the field after rolling over twice it landed on its tyres with the sirens making a sound like a strangled cat.

We pulled to a halt and I shouted to jay to call an ambulance, I leapt out of the car and through the broken fence towards the smashed up police range rover, as I approached the vehicle to very shaken police officers emerged from the vehicle, the female police officer who had been driving had a few cuts and bruises and shock had set in, she kept shouting is every body ok, I told her to calm down and that no body else was injured just shook up, I found some tissue to stem the blood from the cuts on her hand , within minutes all hell let lose first an ambulance appeared and then it was like a scene from the key stone cops, there were more coppers than soft Mick all milling around and each of them astounded that the two coppers in the vehicle had got

out with only a few cuts and bruises, our details were taken and we made our way home to await statements being taken.
When we got home I still couldn't believe that had we been on the road 10 seconds earlier we would have been wiped out.

I can only think that my guardian angel was defiantly there that day and that it wasn't my time to vacate this world.

You were coming up to your last year in primary school and had been child minded by carol and Alan Hines since you were 6 months old We had trusted carol to look after you and for most of the time she did a pretty good job, the problem was that as you got older you got more and more independent and carol took advantage of this most of the time you were left to look after the other kids the she cared for whilst she sat on her fat arse reading the latest copy of my weekly, me and your mum had raised our concerns with each other about this but thought that as you only had a few months until you left primary school we would hold our tongue and stay nothing.
It was one day when I called to pick you up that Alan asked me did I fancy going out for a chat and few beers. I agreed to meet him the following Friday in Manchester. When I walked into the pub I was a little taken aback at the young lady that was sat next to him, a 20 something year old with legs up to her arm pits and long blond hair, within a few minutes it was plainly obvious that he was having an affair and that I was being used as his alibi. As you can imagine I wasn't best please to be used in this way, having been friends for 20 years I thought that this was taking the friendship a little to far, I eventually called Jay and asked him to pick me up. Alan borrowed £30.00 from me to pay for the bimbos taxi home and jay picked us up and dropped Alan off at home, after dropping Alan off jay asked me what had happened and why I had decided to come home so early, I told him of the evenings events and how pissed off and used I felt. Jay said that he didn't trust Alan what so ever and my revelations didn't surprise him in the slightest.

Looking at carol the following Monday morning I felt sorry for her I know she wasn't the brightest button in the box, a little dumpy and slow but even she didn't deserve what Alan was doing to her,
I told Alan that we had been spotted out in Manchester whilst crawling from pub to pub and the person who had spotted us knew both him and Carol and that he should end it before it went to far, he then told

me that the blond he had been seeing had a boyfriend who that same morning had asked her who Alan was? She denied all knowledge of his question and her boyfriend then said that she had been talking in her sleep and kept mentioning Alan's name. Needless to say he stopped it immediately.

The following Monday I called at carols to pick you up but the house was empty, I drove up the road to the shop to see if you were there , I then called at her mothers down the road , but I couldn't find you, in desperation I called your mum and questioned her as to weather I had got my days mixed up and was I actually having you that night, you mum confirmed that I was having you and that you should be at carols house, a guy a cross the road said that he thought you might be further down the road as the child of one of her friends was having a party, I knocked on the door and to my relief carol answered the door " fucking hell she replied cant I go over the road for a brew without you banging on the door " she snarled at me , I was fuming at her tone of voice get your things Laura and get in the van I said.
Carol returned to the house , threw Laura's bag at her and again started to rant and rave at me , I told her in no uncertain terms that I was appalled at her behaviour and that laura would not be coming her again.
A few minutes later, Alan phoned me and in his smarmy manor told me to go back to carol and apologise to her. ME apologise, I don't think so, I slammed the phone down and called your mum. She told me not to worry as she would sort out somebody else to look after you.
I called Alan later that evening and told him that Laura would not be returning to be looked after by carol and that I was appalled at the way both of them had treated me .
He told me that he had always treated me with respect and didn't know what I was talking about. I happened to mention the little matter of the blond bimbo that he had been shagging that his precious wife knew nothing about and his tone of voice soon changed.
I wrote to carol the next day informing her of the immediate termination of the childminding contract we had with her and informed her that I felt her totally unfit to look after a dead budgie let alone children and would be reporting her to offstead., I indirectly wrote about the affair her slimy husband had been having behind her back , but knew that she was to thick to read between the lines and wouldn't have a clue.

I received a hand delivered letter the following day from supposedly from carol telling me she had read the letter in full and Alan had told her everything… the letter actually came from Alan who had picked it up prior to carol seeing it , he had taken it to work and wrote a reply supposedly from carol on the works p.c. the give away was the wording he used but most of all Carol the silly cow can just about read and write let alone use a computer.
I was furious that he thought I could be that stupid. I followed a reply to carol only attaching the letter she had supposedly written and posted it to her after he had gone to work. Now that would have put the cat amongst the pigeons. Lol.. a few weeks later when we were shopping in Asda they were coming down the isle that we were going up and they left the shopping in the middle of the store and went out of the door, Strange I thought, did he not want me to talk to her .

Now that's what I call power!! Or was it damage limitation on his part.

Christmas 2004 came and went and we went into 2005 looking forward to another great year, the landscape out of the picture window at home changed on a daily basis. It was like having a live picture on the wall that was never the same any day of the year.

In the December of this year I was going to be 40. The thought of being forty had filled me with dread so I decided to throw the biggest birthday party to date that I had ever thrown.

This party was not just a party to celebrate my 40th but it would be the first time that all my family and friends would be under 1 roof since I had changed my life from being "straight" to living a gay life. It was going to be my way of firstly saying hey!! Welcome to my life and secondly to say thank you to my friends for not judging me but most of all for all the support I have had from them over the past 5 years and last but not least to celebrate my 40th.

As I was adamant I was not going to be 40 I decided that I would have a 35th birthday. I set to writing a list of all the people I wanted to be there, this wasn't hard at all, the next thing I decided to do was send all my guests a pre invite letter.

Pre invite letter

Hi guys,

On December 7th 2005 it will be my "35th" birthday and I will be having a party.
The party will be held on Friday 2nd of December 2005 (book this date into your diary now!! (Well go on get a pen and do it now or you will forget)

Your invitation will be sent to you in august make sure you keep it safe as you will have to produce it on the night, the reverse will have a map of the venue and all the details you will need.
Make sure that you are not late as if you are you wont be allowed in. For those of you who have had the privilege to attend one of our party's within the past 2 years you will know that this party is not to be missed.
This pre invite letter is to let you know of the date, therefore allowing you to do any of the following, these will be to rearrange or cancel any of the following.

Holidays,
If already booked, cancel and rearrange.

Childminders and baby sitters,
Book them now or put your kids in a care home for the weekend, palm them off with the in-laws or lock them in the garden shed.

Pets.
Leave them to ruin your home, look after your kids or palm them off with somebody who isn't privileged enough to receive an invite.

Work, overtime or shifts.
Book the time off now or arrange to throw a sickie, you have plenty of time to think of an excuse, I will be available if you need any help or ideas on excuses, as I have used them all in the past.

Christmas parties.
Don't bother going to one on December 2nd! As it will be boring and you will be spending time with people you work with and to be honest don't really like, you will end up snogging somebody you don't know and spend the next 12 months feeling guilty about it.

Any other boring or less inviting parties you have invites for cancel them now and make all the excuses you have to do as you wont be going to them as they will not be patch on the party you will be coming to.
This is one party you do not want to miss.

Regards love and hugs

P.J.XX

As all the pre invite letters had been sent out, I set my mind to finding a venue for the party, I looked at numerous places but they were either to small or to grotty, yea!! I know I am a snob but I had make sure that the venue was perfect I didn't want to leave anything to chance and this party had to be perfect
Eventually I went to the Mossley Masonic hall and the place was perfect, I booked the room for the 2nd of December and received menus to look over.

I spent hours and hours on the Internet sourcing balloons, and table decorations and then the paper for the invites.

With all this in place I started to write the thank you speech that I would "perform" on the night. You may think that it was a little early to start thinking about the speech but I had so many people to thank and so many things to say that knew it would take me nearly 12 months to perfect it.

As September approached I received a text from Will, his text upset me as it basically pointed out that he had found the love of his life but couldn't have him.
I took the bull by the horns and called him on the phone.

This was only the second time I had ever spoken to will. The first being a quick hello and that was that.
To hear his voice was fantastic and our 20-minute conversation surrounded the situation he was in at the present time.

Even though it was very normal talking to him it was a little strange, as I had never met him in the past 7 years we had been communicating.

I suggested that I thought it was time I met him for the first time and didn't want our first meeting to be at my party.
Will told me that money was a little tight but that didn't faze me at all I arranged to send him the fare for the journey down hear, after all I owed him so much moor that a train fare I owed him my life.

On my return from work I mentioned to Jay about Will coming down and he agreed, I also understood that this must be quite strange for jay, after all even though I had never kept will a secret I could understand that he may be a little wary and dubious about the guy.

I will clearly point out at this stage that the friendship I have with will is clearly that, a friendship. It has never been and never would be anything other than that.

Neither Will or I can understand our friendship and neither of us have dissected it or tried to work it out, we just accept it for the friendship that it is.
Had Will been just a "shag" it would have happened 7 years ago and more than likely the friendship would never have lasted.

We arranged for will to come down the weekend of
………………………… and like most of the other weekends we continued to look for a shirt that I could wear for my 35th party.
I didn't want just any old shirt I wanted something that looked classy. We had spent the past few weeks shopping in Manchester city centre, the Trafford centre. The Lowry outlet mall Leeds, Stockport, Oldham, Hyde, Denton, and anywhere else we could think but all to no avail, I still couldn't find a shirt I wanted.

As the Friday approached Will's train was arriving at 7pm at Piccadilly station, jay was cooking a meal for us and I was to go and pick up will from the station.

I arrived home from work and made sure that everything was in its place, I had prepared all the food for cooking got showered and changed and waited for jay to come home.

Jay informed me that he would come with me to the station, this made me chuckle to myself, like I said before he must have been apprehensive in his mind about this guy he had never met but who his partner spoke about a lot and told him so much about his life. In jays eyes if he came to the station to pick up Will with me this way "we couldn't get up to anything on the journey from the station to getting home"

As we arrived at the station I got a txt from Will to say that his train was just pulling into the station and that he would meet me on the concourse, we parked the car and jay asked me did I know what Will looked like…..No I said, the look of amazement on jays face was a picture, he asked me how the bloody hell I was going to find somebody on a station concourse on a busy Friday night that I didn't know what he looked like.
I just told him that I would no him when I saw him his reply was I cant wait to see this.

As we approached the station concourse there must have been at least a thousand people on the concourse going about there business we made our way across the concourse and then I spotted this guy stood by one of the fast food outlets, instinct told me that this was Will, I approached him and simultaneously we both said its been a long time in meeting you. I gave him a hug and introduced him to jay.

Jay was amazed that I instantly could recognise my friend having never met him and only twice spoken to him on the phone, having spent the past 7 years talking to this guy and knowing all about him I knew that I would recognise him in a crowd; he spoke, looked and behaved just as I had imagined he would.

We returned home and jay set about making dinner,

We sat for hours talking about the events of the past 7 years, filling in the few blanks that had been left out and swapping photos of family members, it was great to be able to put a face to the people that Will had talked about for so many years and admittedly touching and very moving when he showed me a picture of Jo, his sister that had been killed.

It must have been gone 4 in the morning before we said our good nights. The following morning, I cooked a full breakfast before we made our way to the Trafford centre, for years in many of my letters and e-mails I had told Will that when he came to Manchester I would take him to the Trafford centre, and seven years later we were on our way.

After a days shopping in the Trafford centre and with me still looking for a shirt for the party of the century we returned home to chill for an hour or two before getting changed and heading in to Manchester for a meal and a few drinks.

Meeting Will after all this time was one of the warmest feelings I have ever had, we had travelled through such an emotional few years together, each one of us trying in vain to come to terms with the roller coaster of feelings, emotions and hurt that we had both been subjected to and both of us coming out the other side as "normal" human beings, but most of all to stay as friends was a feat in its self.

By the way!! I have for many years looked for the meaning of the word "normal" and I have come to the conclusion that Normal dose not exist.
What is Normal for one person is far from Normal for another.

Prior to dropping Will off at the station we headed in the central Manchester to do a little moor retail therapy, jay has always had a fascination with the top floor of Kendal's with there electric gadgets and large screen televisions. Whilst in store I picked the 2005 Kendal teddy bear and a thank you card as a small gift from jay and myself to say thank you for a great weekend.

We dropped Will off at the station said our good bys and headed off home.
The journey home was quiet and in some way a bit of an anti climax, having met my friend of 7 years and covered so much in less than 48 hours. With plenty of laughter and even tears I felt down and didn't want the weekend to finish. I was glad that jay had met Will but still felt that he didn't truly believe that we were just friends. I think his problem like many others who knew of our friendship was that they tried to work it out; the best way is to leave it alone and not to rip it to bits and read to much into it.

The next time I would see Will, would be at my 35th party, and time was running out to firstly find a shirt that I felt comfortable in and also to finish all the minor details for the night.

We had been invited to a party at a friend of carol Stafford's, I had been a friend of Carols for a number of years and first got to know her when I started to do her garden for her, I liked Carole for the pure fact that she calls a spade a spade and has worked hard to become a fantastic business woman, finding a niche in a difficult market and being down on her luck with a family to support she spent hour upon hour making her business work.
Her friends Carole and Wayne lived in Glossop, to be bluntly honest I didn't really like either of them and purely for the fact that they didn't really like us, on this particular evening and always felt that we were the token gay friends that had to be invited to a party to make it look like they mixed in all the best circles, you have to remember that at this time its very "FASIONABLE" to have gay friends.??

At this party we met Gail and debs a gay couple who were pleased that they weren't the only 2 gay people at the party, we got on quiet well and debs had been married before she came out, so we had a little in common but being honest they were a little strange,
Gail reminded me of the character Frank Gallagher from the shameless TV program and debs reminded me of Thelma from Scooby doo

After the party they asked us if they wanted us to meet them in Manchester the following Saturday for a few drinks, we agreed and met them the following week. Whilst we were out we were talking about my party and debs told us of their friend who was a drag artist come DJ and if we were interested we could meet up with her later that night. After a few drinks we met up with Miss Melanie,

I must have been pissed because apart from a good sense of humour she actually looked quite nice??
I mentioned my party and she/he agreed that she would be my D.J and look after all the music and running of the evening. We agreed that before the party they would come over and discuss what music and the way the night should run. She told me that normally she charged £300.oo per night but as I was a friend of Gail and Debs she

would call it £100.00, with a hand shake we called it a night and made our way home.

The following morning and in the cold light of day reality hit home …. I had just hired a drag queen to host my "35th" Birthday party and had no idea how good or bad he/she really was, but it was to late in the day to change it and to be honest I was looking forward to welcoming my friends and family to (for want of a better word) my world.

The invites were eventually printed and sent out and having exhausted every shop in Manchester and the surrounding areas looking for a shirt for the party I needed to extend my search.
I made arrangements to meet up with Will and eventually traveled to Lincoln to continue with our previous catch up when he was in Manchester and to see if I could find a shirt, hey!! Believe me if you're pissed off reading about this bloody shirt you should have been in Jays shoes looking for it!

I arrived in Lincoln around 9.30 in the morning and was met at the station by Will, I hadn't told jay that I was going to Lincoln as I knew he would have pulled his face about me being alone with Will, Jay had a somewhat air of jealousy about him, and looking in from the outside, I could see that he would be a little unsure about him, but having met him I had hoped that the jealousy would have subsided.
We went for coffee and then continued the conversation from where we left off a week or so earlier, whilst talking Will showed me around Lincoln it was like I had been hear before, having heard so much about Lincoln over the years in all the letters I had received from him the places he showed me lived up to the images I had created inside my mind.
Whilst chatting we continued to walk around the shops to find, (yep you guessed it) the bloody shirt. We walked into a designer boutique and low and behold there was the shirt!, as bold as brass just hanging on a hanger. I asked if they had it in my size, and went to try it on
The fit was perfect, but most of all the cufflinks were engraved with the inscription U R U, to me it was just meant to be in my eyes it spoke volumes.

The shirt cost me £ 65.00 this was the most I had ever spent on a single item of clothing in my life. But compared to the rest of the money I had spent on the party it was nothing and well worth it.

We finally went to see Lincoln cathedral, a stunning piece of architecture that played a special part in will's life.
With the day coming to an end I made my way to the station for my journey home I said my good buys and boarded the train with my new shirt and just my thoughts for company

Both my meetings with Will were not at all strange, having corresponded for such a long time with each other we both new so much about each others lives and had travelled each others journey, and felt the pain and hurt we had both been through, nobody could and would ever be able to work out our friendship, but neither of us worried about anybody's concerns or worries our friendship was unique and like I have said so many times through out this book I owe Will my life.

The next few weeks were a little hectic; I was coming to the end of the maintenance for the business along with putting the final touches to the party.
The replies to the invites that had been sent out were coming in thick and fast and Jay and myself had arranged to cook dinner for Gail, debs and "Miss Melanie" the drag artist I had booked in my pissed up drunken state a few months earlier. They turned up on the Saturday night and I can honestly say that it was one of the strangest meals that I had ever attended, when we met "miss Melanie" she was made up in full make up high heals and wig, Miss Melanie turned up with Gail and debs wearing a pair of track suit bottoms and a jogging top, they walked in to the house and for the life of me I couldn't get my head around this guy that stood in front of us. He looked stunning as a woman but a fucking mess as a bloke, That's probably why he dragged it up…. Well you never know do you.

Over the course of the evening we discussed the way I wanted the evening to run along with the music both jay and I wanted playing, as everthing was sorted we said our good buys and looked forward to seeing them on the night.
I made the final preparations with the Masonic hall regarding the catering, and put the final touches to the speech.

The final invite replies came in and I was very hurt and annoyed that my brother peter and his girlfriend Mandy had made alternative arrangements and were unable to come and that my sister Ann and her husband had thrown there toys out of the cot and decided not to come because I had failed to invite her precious kids to the party.
I had made a conscious decision not to invite any kids as I didn't want the little bastards running around the dance floor like a heard of demented wart hogs high on speed and pretending to be bloody aeroplanes and knocking drinks out of peoples hands.
But apart from that it was an adult night and had adult content and would not be suitable for her kids, had her kids been invited she would have spent the entire evening complaining that the content of the evening was unsuitable for her little darlings and was detrimental to there well being

As for my sister Colette I didn't bother sending her an invite! You have probably guessed by now that I have a desired hate for her and didn't want her presence at my party, and to have my friends having to endure her tails of how ill she was or what body part ached today, or how "one lives in the country"

With the annoyance subsiding I thought fuck it !! Your loss and not mine what hurt me most of all was the fact that this was the only time in my life I had ever asked any thing from them and peter and Ann had blatantly, and conscientious made a decision to boycott my party, well they will need me before I need them and when the time comes they will have to do some serious grovelling.

FRIDAY DECEMBER 2ND 2005.   ITS PARTY TIME…………………..

The past twelve months had in a strange way been exciting as well as hectic and organising the party had taken up almost every spare minute I had, at no stage did I ever think that no body would turn up.

Will arrived early afternoon and we started to finalise the arrangements for the party.
By 5 o'clock we had been to the Masonic hall and decorated the tables with florescent pink and jet black helium balloons waited down with gold boxes, we filled the dance floor with another 50 or so multi coloured balloons and set off back home to get changed, I made a quick detour to the barbers to have a Turkish shave and headed back to the house. When I got home Pat and Eddie had arrived and were busy getting changed, jay had gone to pick his mum up from her house and I eventually showered and changed and put on my new shirt and pants and spent another few minutes going over my thank you speech.
I must admit that I looked good and the shirt was fantastic.(like I have always said, complement yourself as you never know when anybody will pay you a complement)
We made our way to the Masonic hall where my guests had already stared to arrive, I had a little laugh to myself at the thought that people were actually taking the invite seriously and didn't want to be late for fear of having to pay a forfeit.

Once inside the place looked stunning, Miss Melanie and Gail and Debs had already started setting there equipment up Miss Melanie was dressed in a Little Black dress high heals and wig, I must say that she looked the part.
By 7.30 pm my guests had arrived and I spent my time doing the usual mingling and thanking my guests for the cards and gifts.
It was about 8 pm when Miss Melanie introduced herself and informed them that I had a few words to say before the night got under way.

After a little dutch courage I took centre stage and started to read the speech that had taken me nearly 12 months to write.

My speech:

HI Guys...........

YOU LOOK MORE NERVOUS THAN ME ....SO YOU SHOULD.

I CAN SEE YOU SCRUB UP QUITE WELL WHEN YOU TRY,
BY THE LOOK OF IT MATALAN HAS DONE A ROARING TRADE THIS WEEK LOOK AT ALL THE CHEEP POLYESTER HEAR TONIGHT

UNACCUSTOMED AS I AM TO PUBLIC SPEAKING I WOULD JUST LIKE TO SAY A FEW WORDS, ON A TOTALLY WITHOUT PREJUDICE BASIS OF COURSE.

I WOULD LIKE TO SAY A VERY BIG THANK YOU TO EVERY BODY FOR COMING TONIGHT, AND TO THANK YOU FOR YOUR GIFTS AND CARDS WHICH ARE VERY MUCH APPRECIATED I WOULD LIKE TO THANK EVERYONE WHO HAS TRAVELED FROM MILES AWAY TO BE HEAR
I ALSO KNOW WHAT AN HONOR AND PRIVILEGE IT MUST BE FOR YOU ALL TO ATTEND SUCH A PRESTIGIOUS EVENT.

OVER THE PAST FEW MONTHS I HAVE BEEN ASKED A FEW QUESTIONS. FIRSTLY AS I DON'T DO BIRTHDAYS WHY THE HELL AM I HAVING A PARTY AND SECONDLY WHY A 35TH.

AS MOST OF YOU KNOW AROUND 6 YEARS AGO I LOST THE PLOT GOOD STYLE I AND. TO BE HONEST I LIKED LOOSING THE PLOT SO MUCH I STAYED AT 35 BECAUSE I DON'T REMEMBER IT BUT MOOR TO THE POINT LOOKING AT YOU LOT TONIGHT AND SEEING WHAT PEOPLE LOOK LIKE WHEN THEY GET TO 40 (Mr. TAYLOR) HAS CONVINCED ME TO STAY AT 35

THE REASON FOR THE PARTY IS THAT IT GIVES ME THE PERFECT OPPORTUNITY OF GETTING ALL MY FRIENDS UNDER 1 ROOF TO SAY THANK YOU. TO THANK YOU FOR YOUR FRIENDSHIP AND ESPECIALLY YOUR SUPPORT

THE PAST 40 YEARS HAVE BEEN A JOURNEY, WITH SOME VERY HAPPY AND FUNNY TIMES, TIMES THAT I NEVER WANTED TO END AND ALSO SOME VERY UNHAPPY TIMES WHERE SUICIDE WAS A CLEAR OPTION.
WITHIN THE PAST 6 YEARS I HAVE RIDDEN THE MOST EMOTIONAL ROLLER COASTER RIDE I HAVE EVER RIDDEN IN MY LIFE AND WITHOUT YOU GUYS WHO ARE HEAR TONIGHT I WOULD NEVER HAVE COME OUT THE OTHER SIDE. EACH AND EVERY ONE OF YOU HAVE IN SOME WAY SHAPE OR FORM HELP STRUCTURE MY LIFE AND ALLOWED ME TO BE THE PERSON I AM TODAY WITHOUT PREJUDICE OR JUDGMENT. YOU HAVE ALLOWED ME TO BE ME AND TO BE ABLE TO WAKE EVERY MORNING WITHOUT HAVING TO PUT ON A MASK TO FACE THE WORLD AND FOR THAT I THANK YOU ALL VERY MUCH
I WOULD JUST LIKE TO SPEND A FEW MINUTES TO SAY SOME PERSONAL THANK YOU'S

I WOULD LIKE TO THANK MY MUM FOR HAVING SUCH A FANTASTIC AND WONDERFUL ELDER SON, ALSO FOR THE WAY YOU BROUGHT US UP AND FOR YOUR SUPPORT, I KNOW THAT IT WAS NEVER EASY FOR YOU AS WE GREW UP AND UNDERSTAND THAT THE OTHERS WERE NO ANGELS AND I WAS OF COURSE 100% PERFECT.

THANK YOU TO KATHY MY SISTER FOR COMING TONIGHT, ITS JUST A PITY THAT ANNE AND PETER HAD TO MAKE THEIR EXCUSES

A BIG THANK YOU TO GRETA FOR ACCEPTING ME INTO YOUR FAMILY AND ALLOWING ME TO BRIGHTEN YOU LIFE, I KNOW THAT YOU LIFE WAS A LITTLE DULL BEFORE I CAME ALONG BUT NOT ANY MORE DARLING.

I WOULD LIKE TO THANK SCOT, ADELE AND PAUL FOR THE LONG TERM LOAN OF A SECOND MUM, I KNOW THAT THE LOAN WAS NEVER OFFERED AND I JUST TOOK IT AND I ALSO KNOW SCOT THAT IT BRASSED YOU OFF TOTALLY FOR A LONG TIME THAT I CALLED YOUR MUM MY MUM. BUT I THANK YOU FOR BEING A FIRST CLASS GUY AND A GOOD MATE AND FOR ALLOWING ME TO SHARE ONE OF THE MOST IMPORTANT THINGS IN YOUR LIFE. …. YOUR MUM. YOU WILL NEVER KNOW HOW IMPORTANT THIS WAS THEN AND STILL IS TODAY.

I WANT TO SAY THANK YOU TO ELLEN, WHO I HAVE ALWAYS CALLED MY SECOND MUM FROM BEING VERY YOUNG. YOU NEVER REPLACED AGNES BUT WITHOUT YOUR LOVE AND SUPPORT IN SO MANY WAYS OVER THE YEARS AND THE WAY YOU MAKE ME LAUGH AND THE WAY YOU ARE JUST YOU AND ALWAYS THERE FOR ME I THANK YOU.

I WANT TO THANK LYN AND VIJAY FOR JUST BEING YOU AND FOR ALWAYS BEING THERE FOR ME, EVEN IF YOU CAN PLAY TEN PIN BOWLING BETTER THAN ME VIJAY ALWAYS REMEMBER YOU MAY OWN THE BLOODY HOUSE BUT THE GARDEN IS MY DOMAIN SO KEEP OUT OF IT AND STOP PISSING ABOUT WITH THE LAWN

THANKS TO RIC AND LISA FOR YOUR SUPPORT AND FOR THE COUNTLESS TIMES THAT RIC HAS PULLED ME OUT OF THE SHIT WITH WORK.

I WANT TO THANK BAZ AND BRENDA!

I PUBLICLY APOLOGIES FOR ALL THE TIMES I HAVE DISRUPTED YOUR PRECIOUS FOOTBALL BAZ, FOR BURNING YOUR TORCH ON A BONFIRE RENDERING IT TOTALLY USELESS, FOR BREAKING YOUR SHOWER AND FOR HACKING YOUR ROSES DOWN TO GROUND LEVEL, I APOLOGIES FOR ALL THE TIMES I BLED ON THE UPHOLSTERY OF YOUR CAR WHEN YOU TOOK ME TO HOSPITAL ON COUNTLESS OCCASIONS AFTER THE MANY ACCIDENTS I HAD,

THE BEST COMPLIMENT I HAVE EVER BEEN PAID CAME FROM YOU, " I ALWAYS KNEW HE WAS DIFFERENT BECAUSE HE DIDN'T LIKE FOOTBALL"

BREN! THANKS FOR YOUR WORDS OF WISDOM AND THE GALLONS OF TEA AND THE HOURS OF CHAT AND YOUR CONSTANT SUPPORT. ALONG WITH YOUR LOVE AND THE LANG TERM LOAN OF A GARAGE.

I AM SORRY I KILLED YOUR RABBIT BUT THE BLAME MUST REALLY LIE WITH KELLY AND JODY. BUT I WANT TO THANK YOU SO MUCH FOR ALLOWING ME TO VENT MY ANGER AS MS EVENS. WHO I MIGHT ADD HAS HAD A NERVOUS BREAKDOWN HAS FLED THE COUNTRY AND LIVES ON A DESERT ISLAND AND HAS A CONSTANT FEAR OF THE WORDS ON A TOTALLY WITHOUT PREJUDICE BASIS AND THE HFC BANK.

I NEED TO SAY A VERY BIG THANK YOU TO FRED FOR BEING A FANTASTIC GUY AND A WONDERFUL MATE THANK YOU SO MUCH FOR THE HOURS AND HOURS YOU ALLOWED ME TO BORROW YOUR WONDERFUL WIFE WHEN I NEEDED MY BEST CRITIC AND A SHOULDER TO CRY ON AND SOMEBODY TO BASICALLY JUST GET PISSED WITH, I HAVE REPAID YOU THESES FAVORS ON MANY MANY OCCASIONS BY NOT ALLOWING YOUR WIFE TO FILL THE EMPTY BEDROOMS UP WITH SERVICE USERS AND REST BITE PATIENTS, FOR THE AMOUNTS OF DECORATING HOVERING WASHING UP AND CHRISTMAS DECORATION PUTTING UP I HAVE CARRIED OUT OVER THE YEARS WHEN ALL I DID WAS CALL INF FOR A BREW.

I STILL APOLOGIES FOR PUNCTURING YOUR CEILING WITH A KITCHEN FORK WHEN YOU HAD A LEAK AND FLOODING YOUR BUNGALOW BUT I TRULY BELIEVE THAT

YOU SHOULDN'T HAVE LEFT THOSE TWO WAYWARD CHILDREN ALONE IN THE HOUSE AND SECONDLY BELIEVE YOU DID VERY NICELY OUT OF THE INSURANCE…A LARGE G AND T WHEN YOU GO TO THE BAR MATE…
A VERY SPECIAL THANKS TO GILL MY WONDERFUL FRIEND AND MY BEST CRITIC WHO WITHOUT YOU GILL THE DECISIONS I HAD TO MAKE WOULD HAVE BEEN THE WRONG ONES, YOU HAD THE TIME TO LISTEN TO ME AND SHOW MW THAT I AM NOT ALWAYS RIGHT (EVEN THOUGH I AM) AND MY DECISIONS HAD A POWERFUL IMPACT ON NOT JUST MY LIFE, WITHOUT YOUR GUIDANCE I WOULD HAVE HURT PEOPLE MORE THAT WAS NECESSARY I WILL BE FOR EVER IN YOUR DEBT. … I AM SORRY TO HEAR THAT OVER THE COURSE OF TIME YOU HAVE HAD A NASTY EXPERIENCE WITH A HORSE IN A HAIR SALON, DUG A GRAVE STONE UP IN YOUR BACK GARDEN WITH YOUR OWN SURNAME ON IT AND HAVE REVERTED TO JOINING CELL WITH A WOMAN WHO'S HUSBAND HAS THE IMPRINT OF A STEERING WHEEL ON HIS CHEST.
A VERY SPECIAL THANK YOU TO PAT AND EDDIE FOR YOUR FRIENDSHIP OF 20 YEARS AND FOR SHOWING ME HOW TO DRINK HUMONGOUS AMOUNTS OF ALCOHOL, FOR TAKING ME ON AN 8 HOUR RIDE TO A WEDDING WHERE WE GOT LOST THAT RESEMBLED SOMETHING FROM A CARRY ON FILM AND FOR REMINDING ME THAT PINK LADY IS A WONDERFUL DRINK BUT NOT BEFORE AN 8 HOUR COACH RIDE.

NEARLY 7 YEARS AGO I GOT TALKING TO A GUY WHO OVER THIS PERIOD OF TIME HAS BOURN THE BRUNT OF WHAT THE REST OF YOU HAVEN'T.

WILL, THANK YOU FOR THE PAST 7 YEARS, FOR THE TEX MESSAGES LETTERS AND PHONE CALLS AND E MAILS, ONCE AGAIN I WOULD NEVER HAVE GOT THIS FAR WITHOUT YOU
IT WAS ONLY WHEN I RECENTLY MET YOU FOR THE FIRST TIME DID YOU BECOME REAL AND I REALIZED THE EXTENT OF THE FRIENDSHIP WE HAVE
YOU HAVE BEEN MY PERSONAL COUNCILOR EVER SINCE WE FIRST STARTED CHATTING AND HAVE HELPED ME WHEN I HAVE BEEN AT MY LOWEST EBB AND THOUGHT THAT SUICIDE WAS MY ONLY OPTION WITHOUT YOU I WOULD NOT BE HEAR TODAY YOU A RE A WONDERFUL GUY AND A VERY SPECIAL FRIEND AND MY LIFE IS SO MUCH RICHER FOR HAVING YOU IN IT.
I WANT TO SAY A THANK YOU TO THE NEWEST FRIEND I HAVE MADE OVER THE PAST FEW YEARS YOU ALL KNOW WHO YOU ARE.

I NEED TO SAY A VERY SPECIAL THANK YOU TO LAURA, MY PRECIOUS AND WONDERFUL DAUGHTER FOR MAKING ME SO PROUD AND FOR MAKING ME REALIZE THAT IT REALLY DOESN'T MATTER WHAT YOUR SEXUALITY OR YOUR COLOR IS BUT IN LAURA'S WORDS ITS WHETS INSIDE THAT COUNTS DAD…
A VERY SPECIAL THANK YOU TO MANDY… FOR FIRSTLY ALLOWING ME TO CARRY OUT MY DECISION TO LEAVE AND ALLOWING ME TO BE ME BUT MOSTLY FOR HAVING THE COURAGE TO NOT ONLY HOLD YOUR HEAD UP HIGH BUT FOR CONTINUING TO HAVE ME AS A FRIEND AND FOR YOUR LOYALTY AND SUPPORT

I CAN HONESTLY SAY HAND ON HEART THAT YOU HAVE MORE COURAGE AND BALLS THAN ANY GUY I KNOW; YOU ARE 1 HELL OF A PERSON AND A VERY SPECIAL FRIEND
I WANT TO SAY THANK YOU TO PAUL AND PATRICK, NATALIE SIMON AND TRACEY FOR LOOKING AFTER MANDY YOU WILL NEVER KNOW HOW MUCH THAT MEANS TO ME

LAST BUT BY NO MEANS LEAST I WISH TO SAY THANK YOU TO A VERY SPECIAL GUY… JAY! THE BEST PARTNER ANY GUY COULD EVER ASK FOR NEARLY 4 YEARS AGO I WAS PRIVILEGED TO MEET JAY AND WITHIN THIS TIME HE HAS MADE ME

LAUGH SO MUCH, HE IS THE REASON I GET OUT OF BED IN THE MORNING AND THE REASON I GET BACK IN BED AT NIGHT WE SHARE THE SAME PASSION FOR TRAVEL, GOOD FOOD AND ALCOHOL. I WANT TO SAY THANKS FOR YOUR LOVE AND SUPPORT ESPECIALLY OVER THE PAST 18 MONTHS WHEN MY HEALTH HAS BEEN A LITTLE OFF.
THANK YOU FOR ALL THE HELP YOU HAVE GIVEN ME TO MAKE TONIGHT A SUCCESS, AS I COULD NOT HAVE DONE IT WITH OUT YOU.

I WOULD LIKE TO FINISH BY SAYING THAT IF OVER THE YEARS I HAVE KNOWN EACH AND EVERY ONE OF YOU I HAVE MANAGED TO YOU BACK JUST A FRACTION OF THE FRIENDSHIP THAT YOU HAVE GIVEN ME THEN I AM A VERY HAPPY GUY.
TONIGHT IS FOR YOU GUYS, HAVE A FANTASTIC NIGHT AND WHEN YOU GO TO THE BAR MINE IS A LARGE JACK COKE OR A G AND T I HAVE PLACED SOME CAMERAS ON THE TABLES PLEASE FEEL FREE TO USE THEM DON'T WASTE THE FILM BY CUTTING OFF HEADS OR BY PUTTING YOUR FAT CLUMSY FINGERS IN FRONT OF THE LENS

AFTER 9 MONTHS OF LOOKING THROUGH EVERY SONG AND TRACK I POSSESS THIS SONG IS FOR YOU, IT SAYS ALL THE THINGS THAT I HAVEN'T SAID TONIGHT THE SONG IS BY SHIRLEY BASSEY AND ITS CALLED THANK YOU FOR THE YEARS.

FINALLY ONCE AGAIN THANK YOU AND I WILL LEAVE YOU IN THE MOST CAPABLE HANDS OF THE WONDERFUL MISS MELANIE.

By the time I had finished my speech there wasn't a dry eye in the room. With my speech over and all my thank you's said we continued to carry on with the party.
At some point in the evening jays friend Joanne Williams came over to speak to me and told me how sad it was that since me and jay had been seeing each other that had virtually lost contact with him, she then said to me that wouldn't it be dreadful if jay thought something was going on between will and myself. I was horrified at the vile mass of shit that was spewing from her mouth, I told her that just because she was unable to keep a man she should keep her foul mouth shut and should she decide to cause any trouble she would see the other side of me to which I added was not very pleasant at all.
The remainder of the evening went without a hitch and as it drew to a close family and friends started to say there good buys.
Around 30 people returned to our house to continue drinking and enjoying themselves a few of our friends had an early flight the next morning to Las Vegas where jay and I would be joining them on Sunday.
When we returned to the house the very undesirable Joanne Williams turned her attentions to Will and once again started shit stirring, things started to go horrible wrong and Will ended up outside the front door in floods of tears. I followed him outside to try to ease the situation, I felt terrible as the poor guy knew nobody and this horrible woman was

doing her best to rake up as much shit as humanly possible and ruin the evening as well as our friendship.

Whilst I was outside a guy called Steve came out to stick his two pence worth in to the situation, I told him that this was a private conversation and politely asked him to go inside, he informed me that he was my guardian angel and that he was going nowhere, already wound up like a ticking time bomb I again asked him to go back inside the house where he instantly informed me that he wasn't going any where. I told him that if he didn't go in I would punch him! He very smugly tapped his chin and said you can hit me hear if you want, the time bomb eventually went off and the next thing I knew was my fist was coming into contact with his chin and the only thing running through my mind was the last time I hit somebody and ended up in a police cell.

Eventually we went into the house and Steve decided that he wanted to get his own back and pinned me to the front door and started banging my head against the back of the door , I could hear somebody in the back ground shouting about the tumour in my head and with all the force I could ,muster up the full extent of the time bomb blew.

I flew towards the Christmas tree picking it up and watching like in slow motions as fairy lights fused and tinsel and baubles flew everywhere as I battered the fuck out of Steve with a seven-foot Christmas tree.

I then set about throwing Joanne Williams and Steve out of the house calling them a barrage of insults in the process, Sue the extremely odd next door neighbour took it upon her self to poke me in the chest with her finger and decided to stick her two pence worth in as well she was met with the same wrath of PJ. I later found out that the cheeky fucker had rummaged through some of my presents, found a bottle of wine and presented it as one that she had brought from home.

The last few minutes of my loosing the plot ended up with me and jay having a blazing row, no matter how many times I tried to explain that his precious friend had been shit stirring he would not listen. Pat and Eddie retreated to the spare bedroom and Will cuddled up under the duvet on the futon on the lounge in floods of tears.

The following morning I came down stairs to find that Will was no where to be found. I tried his phone but it was turned off. The lounge

looked like a scene from a battle ground with broken glass a fucked up Christmas tree and shredded tinsel and broken baubles strewn across the floor
I went into the kitchen and in the corner of the dining room in a heap was the remains of the drag artist, half clothed and looking like the preverbal bag of shit, there were the remains of half a dozen crisp packets strewn around him with a half drank bottle of coke and a half drank carton of milk at the side of him.

Pat and eddies came down stairs and said there good buys and left and I started to clean up the mess that was once a clean tidy home ready for our departure for our holiday to Las Vegas.

I called your mum and asked her would she pick me up a new door lock from B&Q as somewhere down the line the door had become fucked in the process, when you and your mum I told her what had happened and just like your mum she took it as the norm. Like I have always said I am the best friend you could ever wish to have but when I am crossed I am your worst enemy.

I spent the next few hours getting rid of the drag artist and cleaning the house, the atmosphere between jay and myself was not pleasant as he refused to listen to the details of what had happened, eventually the cases were packed and we made our way to jays mums to spend the night before our flight to Vegas.
I spent hour upon hour trying to contact Will. I was out of my mind. His phone was still not on and I was increasingly worried about his safety and well-being, he had just left the house obviously very hurt and distressed. It wasn't until around 8 am on the Sunday morning before we flew to Vegas did I eventually manage to speak to him. He was safe and well but like myself felt dreadful about what had happened on the Friday night.
The 11-hour flight to Las Vegas was what you may call a little strained; and to say that there was a "slight chill in the air" was an understatement, most of the flight was spent in silence with only the odd pleasantry passed between us. As we made our final approach to Vegas it is the first time ever we had actually passed our hotel as we came into land.
Vegas is stuck in the middle of the desert and as you come into land you pass all the hotels.

Having cleared all airport legalities we made our way to the Luxor hotel
The shear size and overall look of the whole place just blew you away, we checked into our room and started to explore this amazing fun land that we have flown to, the only thing that I can really say was that it was a very false place.... As you stood outside the Luxor hotel there were two giant sphinx either side of the entrance but when you actually touched them they were made of resin, it soon became clear that all the hotels were as false as each other, don't get me wrong the place was fantastic but like I said it was disappointing as everything was like an adults theme park but false.

By the time we got into bed on the Sunday night, having coped with the difference in the time coupled with the no sleep over the past few nights we had been awake over 50 hours and being honest we were actually totally knackered.
I woke around 4 am in the morning and like every other night looked at the clock and laughed to myself, for the past 30 years it made no difference what time I went to bed I would always wake up at 4.am, I dressed and jay grumbled to me that he hoped that it wasn't 4 in the morning as he liked my company but hated my hours, I told him that I would try to find a coffee some where and that I would see him later.
I left the hotel room and the familiar hum of slot machines and music and voices filled the air I looked over the balcony and to my amazement the place was full of people milling around, drinking and gambling, this place didn't sleep, there were little old ladies sat on stools feeding slot machines with quarters whilst they had there shoes off and there feet resting on the adjoining stool, hundreds of people sat around card tables and roulette wheels spending there hard earned money, the place just buzzed.
I found a coffee shop on the second floor ordered a coffee to take out and set about exploring the hotel and its dozens of shops and outlets selling every thing from food and drink to souvenir tat.

I watched as people gambled hundreds of dollars at a time in the spin of the roulette wheel only to loose it. I found an electronic poker machine took a seat on the stool and feed it a 5$ bill I hadn't got a bloody clue what I was doing but some how I kept winning, one of the many hostess working the floor asked me if I wanted a coffee refill, yes I replied, this was my way of playing a slot machine as you didn't have to leave the machine and your drinks were brought for you. A ploy by the casino's to keep you spending money,

After what seamed only a shot time I collected my winning from the machine in the form of a chitty and made my way over to the cash desk, I had made 54 dollars and felt quite pleased with my little self considering like I said I didn't have a clue what I was doing. I made my way back to the hotel room to be quizzed as to where I had been, "for a coffee I replied why"? That was around 4 am and it's just gone 9 am he said. I explained that I had got caught up on a poker machine and came out 54 dollars better off, Jay got him self ready and we made our way down to reception to meet our friends that had flown out 2 days earlier.

It was great to see del boy, carol and John and del boys friends Alison and Craig, we sat and had coffee and a light breakfast and planned out our day, carol and john were spending time together, Alison and Craig were going to find some more free things to do so we asked del boy to spend the day with jay and myself.

We decide to go to one of the out of town outlet malls to do some retail therapy, we got a cab to the mall and set about firstly find some designer boxer shorts for jay and a coat for myself, I knew that when we flew on to new York it would be minus whatever degrees so I needed a good coat, I found my coat in the timberland shop priced at 65 dollars, the same coat in the timberland shop in the uk was £129.99 so 65 dollars was more than a bargain.

Having spent a few hours shopping we headed back to the Las Vegas strip and into the New York new York hotel, all the hotels are themed and individual in every way shape and form. We made our way to the bar and ordered three beers; Delboy then asked the question of how the remainder of the party went! Jay took great delight in telling her about how I had lost the plot and not only battered Steve with a 7 foot Christmas tree but trashed the house and the Christmas tree in the process, insulted his work colleague and threw them out.

I gave my events of how the problem had started but jay refused to listen to what I was saying, Del boy asked jay about His friend Joanne Williams and the revelations that he told had me totally gob smacked.

It is apparent that in the past Jay and Joanne Williams had worked together and whilst working with each other she had on more than one occasion shit on him from a great height, causing him not only embarrassment at work but also for them to fall out in a big way.

Both myself and del boy could not believe what he was telling us, she had used him, shit on him and caused him embarrassment but he still decided to take her side of the story over mine. This made me feel very hurt and betrayed, and I honestly didn't think I could ever forgive him for what he had done.

The next few days in Vegas was magical as well as exhausting, we visited all the hotels and took in all the sights, I think the most memorable part of the holiday was visiting the fountains at the venation hotel every half hour the fountains dance to pieces of classical music. Hand on heart it's a very moving and memorable experience that I think every body should, if they ever get the chance experience.

At midnight we made our way to down town Las Vegas and on to Fremont Street. As the lights dim we experienced a fantastic light and sound show that blew your mind.

December 7th 2005.

I woke as usual around 4.am and spent the next few hours watching jay sleep.
When he woke we made our way down to the reception and started to flick through the telephone directory for the number of a helicopter company to take us on a flight over the Grand Canyon,.
At two thirty we were picked up from the hotel and made the 20-minute trip to Boulder city airfield, once we had paid for the trip we were led to the helicopter and introduced to our pilot, we boarded the helicopter and started our assent.

This was one of the most exhilarating experiences I have ever had the privileged to experience, we travelled at around 150 miles an hour, but it felt like we weren't moving at all, as we flew over the ridge of the canyon the pure feeling of ....WOW......... swept over my entire body, filling me with such an awesome ecstatic feeling, to be able to see the formation of such a wonderful sight was out of this world,
As we passed over lake bled and took in the sight of the hover dam it was a sight and a feeling that will stay with me for the rest of my life, whilst I write this I have the same feelings that I had 3 years ago, the feeling of the butter flies in the pit of my stomach and the hairs that are standing up on the back of my neck. As we came into land at boulder city the sun had just started to set in the sky and it was one of the best sunsets that I have ever witnessed. God I feel privileged today.

As we made our way back to the hotel my body still tingled and the butterflies were still doing summersaults in my stomach, whilst we got ready to go out for dinner we chatted about the events we have just witnessed.

We met Carol, John, Del boy, Alison and Craig in reception of the hotel and walked to the Mandela bay hotel where we were going for pre drinks before dinner. Carol and john took us up to the 64th floor of their hotel and made our way to the sky bar, a fantastic and funky bar that looked down the complete Las Vegas strip. The views over Las Vegas were breath taking you could pin point every hotel and all the attractions of the wonderful but very bazaar place.

We made our way to the funky forest restaurant on the lower ground floor of the hotel, they tried to palm us off on a cramped little table stuck in the corner of the restaurant, but in true Carole style she wasn't having that, she collared the waiter and informed he that she wanted the very large table in the centre of the restaurant, a few seconds later we were seated at the large round table and dinner was served.

In the 40 years I have been on this earth this had to be the best birthday I had ever had, the company was fantastic, the location was second to none and I was with the partner I loved, respected and cared for so much.

As dinner came to an end carol and john informed me that I had to follow them to the front of the hotel as my birthday present was waiting for me outside.

When we got to the front of the hotel there was a big yellow stretched hummer waiting for us and at our disposal for the next 2 and a half hours.

One again I was gob smacked, we all got in to the hummer and spent the next two and a half hours living like super stars, the jack denials and coke were flowing freely and 80's music boomed out of the open windows.

We stopped at the famous "welcome to Las Vegas" sign, and visited as many sights as we could. This truly was another awesome and thoroughly exhilarating experience.

As our evening came to an end we pulled up at the hotel and said our good nights. Tomorrow was another day!

Its 5 minutes to 12 on December 7th 2005, I have experienced one of the most magical, most sensational and exhilarating experiences in my life today I am 40 years old and it has been the best birthday I have ever had.

Who said that life doesn't begin at 40 ??

This is the end of my first 40 years. Who knows what the next chapter of my life holds?

I would like to spend a few minutes saying a few thank you's to the special people over the past 40 years who have always been there for me.
They are not in order of importance but just like the rest of the book. As it comes............

I would like to say a very special thank you to Sue Duncan Gilbert. Our meetings in your councillors room was the start of my long journey in finding the real me. The compassion time and energy you gave me allowed me to find the person I truly wanted to be but was so frightened and so afraid to let out.
You showed me that I could now remove the mask I had kept firmly in place for years and face the world as a stronger person
You sympathetically allowed me to face the demons that haunted me both by day and night and allowed me to open the box that I had kept chained up and hidden in the back of my mind.
This box contained all the hurt and pain I didn't know how to cope with the abuse and the fear of being once again un- loved and un- wanted.
Having spent nearly 12 months in your company I thank you from the bottom of my heart and look forward to the day I can meet you again as the real me ......Thank you.

Gill.
From the day we first met something clicked, we have always got on so well and I have to thank you for the hour and hours you spent with me. Allowing me to rabbit on and on whilst I tried to muddle through all the confusion that bombarded my brain, you have been not only my true and honest friend but my councillor and confident, your friendship, love and guidance allowed me to see things from not just my point of view but also from Mandy's and Laura's point of view. Without your guidance I would have made so many bad and irreparable mistakes and would have not only lost my daughter but also I would have lost one of the best friends I have the privilege to have, "Mandy".
Your dedication as a friend is impeccable and I thank and love you from the bottom of my heart xx PJ

Fred.
Thanks mate; you're a guy in a million and a true friend. X PJ

Ellen.

Thanks for being my second mum, for your love and friendship and for all the times I needed you, your 1 special lady. Love P.J

Will.

No matter how many times I say thank you it will never ever seam enough, so many people have walked into my life and turned around and fucked off, as in there eyes they could not cope with the reality of the shit I carried about.
You are different. You are 1 of the kindest most sincere guys I have the privilege to be able to call a friend. Over the past 8 years your love and guidance and ability to listen to me without judgment is beyond belief.
Through out this book I have said so many times that without you on the end of the P.C and without the letters of encouragement and support I would have committed suicide. You gave me the hope and the support to not only believe in myself but to be able to carry on when I truly felt that I had nothing else to live for and I was at the lowest part of my life.
I have never tried to analyse our friendship in the fear that if I ever get to the bottom of it, it will cease and I would lose your friendship for ever
I thank you with all of my heart and it is an honour to be able to call you friend, with all my love and thanks. P.J xx

Mandy.

Thank you, thank you, thank you,
I know the past 8 years have been 1 hell of a roller coaster ride for you and inevitably you did get hurt, please be assured that when I met you this was never my intention, from the day I met you I fell in love with you and never stopped loving you. The difference is, is that it's now a different kind of love.
I tried so hard to absorb as much of the pain and the shit to enable you to hold your head up high, I never wanted you to get hurt, you will never know how much hurt I had to absorb just so that you didn't have to suffer any more pain.

You are a remarkable wonderful person with a heart of gold and you will never know how privileged I feel that you still have the guts to call me your friend
Thank you…… love always .PJ XX

Baz and Bren.
 Just thank you for being there? Love P.J XX

Lynn and Vijay.

It's a pity that there not more people like you in this world,
I thank you both for all your support and love over the years and value your friendship more than you will ever know. Xx PJ

Jay.
The past few years have been some of the best times in my life, I am eventually the person I want to be and think I have found the person I wish to spend the rest of my life with.
I know that we have had some ups and downs and truly hope that you will just accept me as the workaholic and the accident prone guy that I am.
I hope that you take the time to read this and may be then your will know some of the shit I have encountered and why I am the person I am today.
Who knows what the next years hold. Like I always said we only shuffle the cards. Life plays then for us, Love always, P.JXX

Laura.

Well my darling I have come to the end of what I can only describe as the longest roller coaster ride of my life, like I said at the beginning of this book it's a very true and honest account of my life.
Maybe now you will be able to understand why I am the person I am today, how the events and people closest to me as detailed in my book have helped me to become the person I am today.

You will never know how much love and respect I have for you and to watch you grow into the young lady that you are today is a wonderful feeling.

As you grow older always remember that your actions always have a consequence,
Never allow anybody to make you feel like I have been made to feel in parts of my life
Even though, I still think that I have somewhere down the line fucked your life up!!!

With all my love hugs cuddles kisses squidges and squeezes.

        DAD XX

Over the years so many people have walked into and out of my life.
The only ones that are still left are the ones that you can count on your fingers.
I am honoured and privileged to call you my friends and have you in my life.

Statement of Intention

I am now turning in to the best of who I am:
the part of **Me** that is loving, giving,
confident, appreciative, Peaceful and patient.

I open my heart and allow loving energy to flow through me.
I am aware that my life makes a difference and that every
action I take helps to heal the hurts within and around me
I move into life knowing there is nothing to fear.

Within me is an endless source of wisdom and strength
that will handle all that needs to be handled. I am being
Shown the way. I move into the light and see the huge
expanse of possibility.

Today I push away all self doubt
and replace it with self trust. I constantly remind myself
My life is unfolding in a perfect way. I trust the grand
Design I am grateful for the opportunity to create love in this
World.

I am listening to the divine within me. I appreciate
All the opportunities this life gives me for becoming
a more caring and compassionate human being.
I am Truely blessed

Printed in Great Britain
by Amazon